Starting in Oils

ROY RODGERS

Series Editor
Ken Howard

BLOOMSBURY

For Cheryl, Alexander, Dominic and Joel

First published in 1988 by
Bloomsbury Publishing Limited,
2 Soho Square, London W1V 5DE

Copyright © Swallow Publishing Ltd 1988

Conceived and produced by
Swallow Publishing Ltd, Swallow House,
11-21 Northdown Street, London N1 9BN

Editor: Anne Yelland
Art director: Elaine Partington
Designers: Stephen Bitti and Glynis Edwards
Photographer: Tim Imrie
Studio: Del and Co.
Printed in Spain by Mateu Cromo

Note: Throughout this book, American terms are signalled
in parentheses after their British equivalents the first time
in each section they occur. In frame and artwork
measurement, height always precedes width.

British Library Cataloguing in Publication Data

Rodgers, Roy
    Starting in oils.——(Art class).
    1. Oil paintings – Manuals
    I. Title   II. Series
    751.45

    ISBN 0-7475-0128-9

Contents

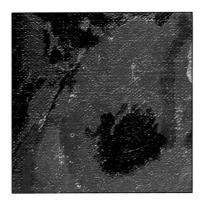

Foreword by Ken Howard 4

Introduction 6

Materials and equipment 10
   Oil paints **10**
   Paintboxes **11**
   Brushes **12**
   Palette knives **13**
   Palettes **14**
   Diluents **14**
   Mediums **14**
   Easels **15**
   Painting supports **16**
   Recommended kit **22**

Starting to paint 24
   Use of brushes **24**
   Laying out your palette **25**
   Colour **26**

Wet into wet **28**
   Glazing **28**
Dragged brush techniques **30**
Using a painting knife **30**
   Scumbling **31**
   The doodle **31**

Project: A still life 1 32

Underpainting 38
   Underpainting technique **38**
Monochrome underpainting **39**

Project: A still life 2 40

Subjects for the oil painter 48
   Painting out of doors **49**
   Using photographs **51**
   Painting from sketches **52**

Composing a picture 54

Index 60
Acknowledgements 60

Foreword

'Has he got a magic brush?'
A little boy who was standing behind me while I was painting outside in oil colour made this remark to his mother; it is probably the most flattering remark I have heard made about my work.

There is always an element of magic in painting and it is this which has fascinated people through the ages, it is this which keeps people flocking to museums and art galleries. However, although it could be said that the most important element in the painting is the magic, like many other creative processes, there

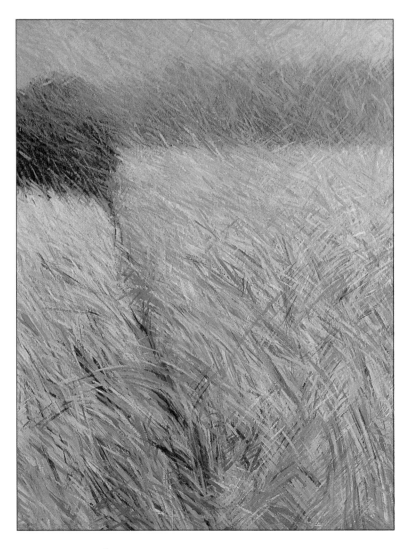

Roy Rodgers 'Grass in Sunlight' 1010 × 760mm (40 × 30½in.). Here, the oil paint has been applied with both brushes and a painting knife. The knife enables a sharp linear mark, well suited to convey the textural qualities of grass.

is much more besides. There is an element of magic in excellent cooking, but cooking involves selecting the various ingredients and using them with imagination and so does painting. This book aims to introduce you to the various ingredients you may wish to use in painting in oils.

Art Class is a series of titles geared specifically to the requirements of the amateur painter. Some of the books are technique-based to help you to acquire first the basic, then the more advanced, techniques you need to enable you to work in a particular medium. Others are subject-based, outlining the theory and principles which you should understand in order to produce pleasing and technically adept works of art. All are full of sound practical advice, and suggest exercises and projects which you can do in order to gain a clear understanding of the subject. All the writers involved in the series, as well as being professional artists, have at some time in their careers been involved in teaching in art schools; indeed I have had the pleasure of teaching with several of them myself.

The most important element of learning to paint is that you must love to do it, you must enjoy it. That does not mean that it will not be difficult and that you will sometimes want to give up, but once you have been bitten, you will always return to try again. As you practise you will get better, and as you get better you will want to practise more, and as you practise more you will get even better.

A very common mistake among people who are beginning to paint is to believe that having done a subject once, that is enough. This of course is quite wrong. If you look at masters such as Chardin, Degas or Morandi you will see that they sometimes pursued the same idea for years. When using a book like *Art Class* there is the danger that having done a project once, one either feels it is done or worse still that one has failed to achieve the desired result. In order to achieve a good result it is necessary to do the projects many times and each time you will find you get nearer to the desired aim.

Roy Rodgers' title, *Starting in Oils*, is full of helpful instruction and knowledge about the process of oil painting of which he has a wide experience both as an exhibiting painter and as a teacher in art schools. He shows oil paint to be a liberating medium, full of varied possibilities and not in the least hidebound by tradition or technique. Read his book, practise what he says time and time again and you will learn the magic in painting in oils.

Ken Howard

Introduction

Oil painting is one of the oldest and most widely used methods of painting, and because of the number of examples reproduced in books and on display in public art galleries, it has become the most familiar way of painting to us. This is probably one of the initial reasons why many people who wish to take up painting choose to work in oils. However once this decision has been made, one quickly realizes that there are many good reasons why the medium has survived for so long – oil has been widely used since the fifteenth century – and retained its popularity in the face of such modern alternatives as acrylics and resin-based paints.

'Frosted Grass' 500 × 600mm (20 × 24in.). This picture shows how the palette knife can be used as an expressive way of making marks which relate to the subject matter, in this case frosty grass. By using the edge of the knife I was able to give that sharp, crisp quality needed to convey the feeling and surface texture of frost on the rather linear shapes of the grass.

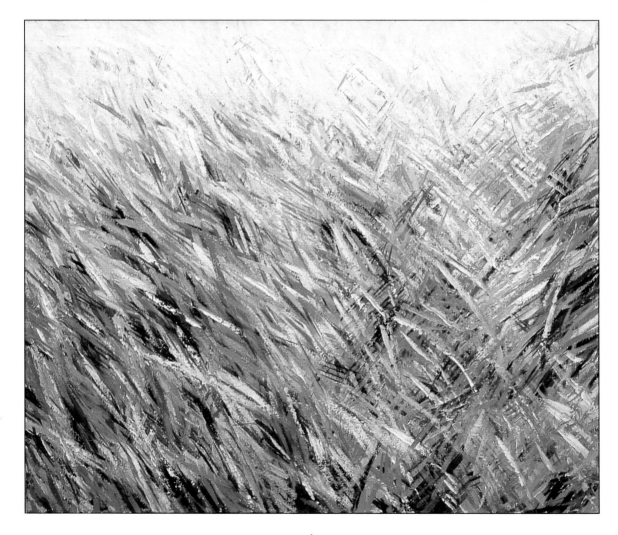

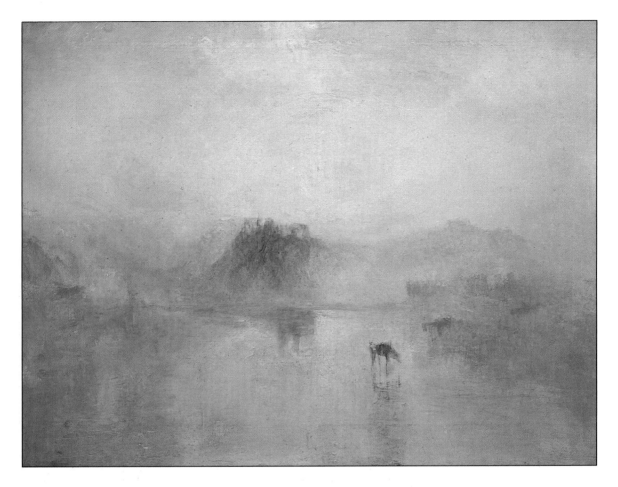

Oil paint is pigment that has been ground in an oil-based medium, usually 'linseed'. The actual pigment is often the same one that is used in watercolour or gouache (body colour or poster paint); it is the preparation that gives it certain unique qualities not present in other paints. Firstly, it tends to impart a richer feeling to the colour. It also makes it a very flexible medium, allowing it to be used in a variety of ways ranging from very thick (called 'impasto') to thin paint which is almost the consistency of watercolour. This also means that the application of oil paint has endless possibilities. It can be applied in almost any way one wishes – by brush, knives, rags and even fingers. There are also notable examples of the paint having been thrown on to the surface.

Although the beginner may feel somewhat intimidated by the long history of oil painting and the high degree of technical craftsmanship of most of the more familiar pictures, due to its flexibility oil paint is, in fact, an ideal medium for the beginner.

J.M.W. Turner 'Norham Castle' 908 × 1219mm (33¾ × 48in.). This beautiful example of painting shows thin transparent paint throughout the whole picture. It has the quality of watercolour which gives the light translucence to the subject. The few impasto areas of paint are reserved for accents of light, catching clouds or water and act as a complement to the thin paint, and give a sparkle within the hazy sunlit atmosphere.

7

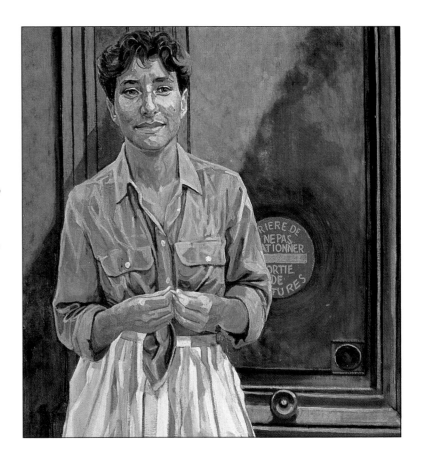

Martin Baldwin 'Portrait of a French Girl' 860 × 610mm (33 × 24in.). In this portrait the artist's careful build up using thin paint on a precise drawing base allows him to explore in detail the smaller forms of the head and drapery. Once the large areas had been broadly laid in, the artist used smaller and finer brushes such as sables for the fine detail. It is a painting which shows that the artist derives obvious pleasure in the pursuit of close observation and carefully modelled forms. Although this example is a portrait, the same approach can be used in any form of painting such as landscape, still life, or even abstract work.

One advantage that it has over most other paints is its drying time, which is considerably longer than water- or acrylic-based paints. This means that one can put the paint on to the canvas, then scrape it off, and work and rework areas of the painting over a much longer period of time.

Oil painting can have a certain air of mystery about it when you come to it as a total beginner, even though you may have worked with other mediums. There is no real reason why this should be so. By applying a practical and logical step-by-step approach to the subject, I will show that anyone who is interested enough to want to try can develop the skills and techniques through which to enhance their natural creativity and enjoy the fresh experience that can be gained by working with oil paints.

The great age of oil painting from which many of the most familiar examples date is probably the Renaissance, although there are also notable Impressionist and Modern paintings. This goes some way to supporting the idea that if the rules are adhered to, the other great quality that oil paint possesses is durability. There are many paintings now hundreds of years old that still retain the freshness of a new work. Sadly there are also many that are in a bad state of decay and preservation due either to neglect or to bad craftsmanship and materials.

There are some good examples of the use of oil techniques set out in these pages, but the most inspirational experience to be had is to go out and look at the real thing. They do not necessarily have to be works by great masters, and while looking at paintings in books can and does whet the appetite, this cannot be compared with the direct experience. No matter how good the reproduction is, you can never really experience fully the textural aspects of the brush or knife marks or the translucent qualities of the paint. By looking at paintings in galleries or museums and seeing and trying to understand how the artist actually executed them, not only will you give yourself hours of enjoyment, but you will also learn a great deal about oil-painting technique.

'Sleeping Dog' 900 × 1200mm (36 × 48in.). This painting gives a feeling of the gestural quality that painting can have. The large format allows the artist to make broad bold marks with large brushes. It is a painting which combines many aspects of applying paint; some has been painted wet into wet, while other areas have brush marks dragged across thick dry paint. The paint has been built up in this way throughout and gives the picture a richness of surface and colour.

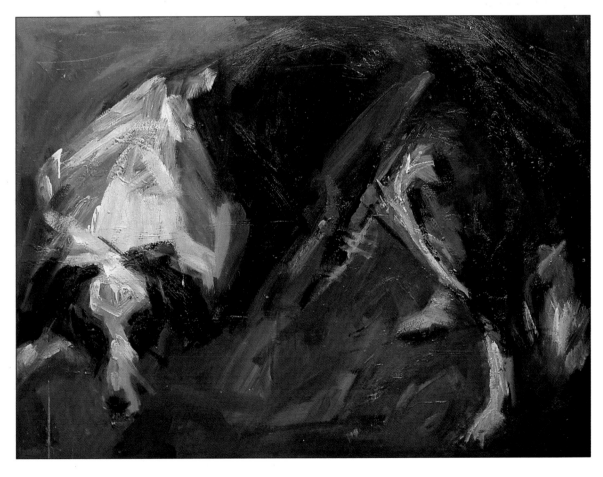

Materials and equipment

The wide range of materials available to the oil painter, most of which are manufactured to a high standard, can be a source of difficulty and confusion for the beginner: where to start? what to choose? how much to spend? In this section, the various materials available and how to use them is outlined and clarified. This will enable you to make choices based on your knowledge of the products and, as you become more experienced, your own personal needs.

Oil colours: (clockwise from bottom left) flake white, cobalt blue, cadmium yellow, cadmium red, viridian, burnt sienna, raw umber, alizarin crimson, burnt umber – all Artists' colours; yellow ochre, terre verte and raw sienna – Students' colours.

Oil paints

Oil paints are produced in two qualities – Artists' colour and Students' colour. Artists' colour is very much more expensive, due to the origin of the pigments themselves: the very best are used in Artists' colours. You will also notice that there is a price variation within the range of colour; this is because of the rarity of some of the pigments, which affects the cost of manufacture. The texture of the paint is also generally smoother, although this is hardly noticeable to the beginner and does not significantly affect the look of the painting.

Tubes of Artists' colour usually have a coding denoting the price range of the particular colour.

Students' colour is manufactured using synthetic dyes and inexpensive pigments as substitutes for the rarer more expensive ones. The texture of these paints is also coarser as the pigments are not as finely ground. Although the Students' range is much cheaper than the Artists' range, there are some colours which are not normally available in it (such as the cadmium colours, cobalt blue and green, and vermilion) because of costs. If you compare Artists' colours with the Students' range you will notice a marked difference in strength and brightness, particularly when mixed with white; Artists' colour will need less to maintain the density of colour.

When you start painting, you will notice that certain colours take longer to dry than others: earth colours dry fairly quickly, while some reds

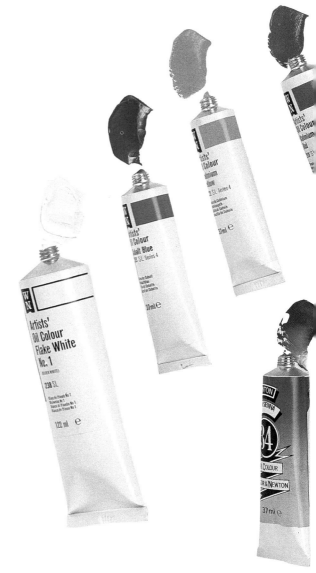

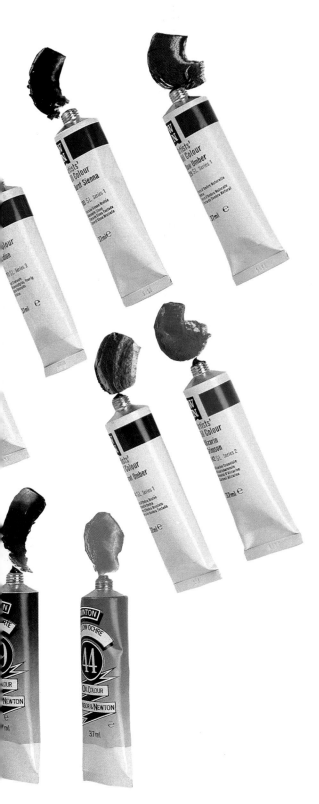

can take three or four days. The earth colours are: yellow ochre, red ochre, raw umber, burnt umber, terre verte, raw sienna and burnt sienna.

With the exception of white (which can be purchased in a large tube), tubes of colour are produced in two sizes. The 37ml (1¼oz./No. 14) size is the most practical for the majority of colours, but because one tends to use far more white than any other colour it is advisable to buy white in the larger (56ml/2oz./No. 20) size. Students' quality paints are also available in 200ml (8oz.) size tins, which unless used fairly quickly will skin over and dry out. They also tend to contain more oil than the tube equivalent.

Having described the basic differences between the two qualities of paint, I think that for the beginner Students' colours are perfectly adequate (to start with). The last thing you want is to feel inhibited by the cost and wastage of your materials, and, at this stage, the difference in results will not be noticeable. However as you progress and gain confidence you can increase your range by adding Artists' colours, as the two types of paint mix perfectly well together. This will also help to keep your initial costs down.

Paintboxes

There are many pre-selected paintboxes on the market. Some of the more expensive ones are beautifully made and can be rather seductive to the beginner. Their big disadvantage, however, is that the selection of colours has been put together by someone else. I think it is important for beginners to make their own selection based on their personal needs and development, and at a realistic cost. Eventually most artists need a container of some sort for all their painting paraphernalia, especially if they paint out of doors. When that time comes the decision will be one of personal preference. You may choose to buy a purpose-made paintbox and supply the materials yourself, or find a convenient-sized plastic or wooden box, or a stout canvas bag to hold all your equipment.

Brushes

There are several types and qualities of brush on the market for the painter to choose from. The most popular brushes for oil painting are bristle made from bleached hog's-hair, and soft brushes made from sable hair. Hog's-hair bristle brushes are fairly stiff, hold the paint well and are manufactured in three different shapes:

Flat brushes have a square-ended shape that is good for applying dabs of colour. If you use the edge, it will give a nice sharp linear mark, useful for drawing.

Round brushes in the larger sizes are good for covering large areas; smaller ones are ideal for initial drawing in.

Filberts are a cross between a flat and a round, except that the shape tapers to a point.

Sable brushes are usually used for detailed work or for thin fine glazes, and they are also ideal for the first drawing in. Some artists prefer to execute a whole painting with this type of brush. These brushes are extremely expensive and unless looked after carefully, they will deteriorate in a very short time. These brushes are not really suited to a rough surface or ground, and will soon show signs of wear if used on one – the hairs tend to become brittle and break off and the brush soon loses its shape.

Synthetic bristle and hair brushes, usually made from nylon, are now also available. They come in the same shapes as the hog's-hair and sable types but are considerably cheaper and for the most part, are very good and hard-wearing. When choosing your brushes it is very much a personal preference, rather in the way that you build up your range of colours. Some artists will use a great many brushes, others will paint with just a few. As a beginner you really need to try various shapes and sizes to enable you to decide what suits your way of working. You may even find that you prefer the synthetic fibre brushes to the more traditional bristle.

The size of the brush is indicated by a number on the handle; the same size numbers do not apply to both hog's-hair and sable brushes, however, so a No. 1 bristle will not be the same actual size as No. 1 in a sable.

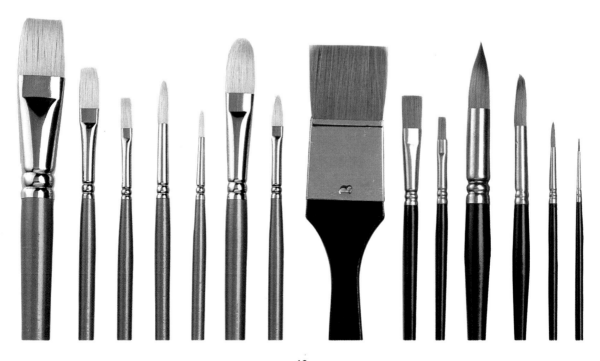

Whereas with paints, you can get away with mixing Students' and Artists' colours, I think that brushes should always be of the best quality from the start. If looked after properly they will last for years and keep their shape.

Brush care

Caring for your brush is of the utmost importance, not only to your pocket but to the quality of your painting. Brushes should be thoroughly cleaned at the end of each day's painting. Wipe the excess oil paint off with a rag or tissue and then rinse with turpentine (white spirit/paint thinner will do for this) until you feel that it is as clean as you can get it. Finally, wash with soap and water by rubbing the brush on to an ordinary household bar of soap and then working up a lather in the palm of your hand. Repeat until the soap suds show no sign of colour and then rinse with warm water. If you shape the brush while it is still wet, when it dries you will find it has kept its shape.

Palette knives

Palette knives have two main functions: applying the paint to the picture surface and scraping it off. It is possible to paint either a part or the whole of the picture with a knife if you desire a rich, textured surface. It is essential for scraping areas of paint from the picture surface to enable them to be reworked if necessary. Its use also extends to mixing colour and cleaning the palette. A wide range of shapes and sizes is available, the choice you make is again (rather like your brushes) a matter of preference. However, you certainly would not need more than one to start with. The most practical type for the beginner is the trowel shape or painting knife, recognizable by its cranked handle and more flexible blade.

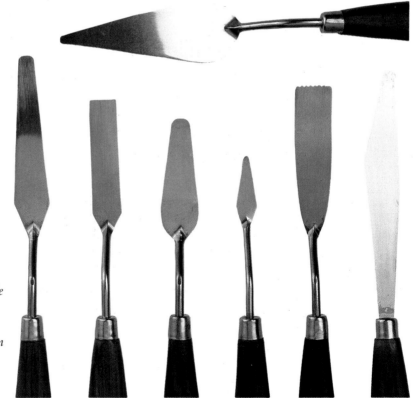

Brushes: (left to right) hog's-hair flats, rounds and filberts of varying widths, large sable wash brush, sable flats and rounds of different sizes.

Right: Palette knives are available in various sizes and shapes – a trowel shape is probably the most practical for a beginner.

Palettes

The first thing to remember about a palette is that it is only the surface on which you set out and mix your paints. There is a wide variety of shapes and sizes available to the artist: you will need to decide at the outset whether you wish to hold the palette or rest it on the table or on some other convenient flat surface.

Most palettes are made to be held, and have a hole for the thumb. They come in two main shapes: kidney shape, sometimes called a studio palette, and rectangular shape. Rectangular ones are usually smaller and will fit into a paintbox. More expensive ones are usually made from mahogany but there are many made from other woods, from plastic or even from paper.

It is not essential to have either of the traditional shapes as long as you have a clean smooth surface. As you will find for most of your basic materials, there are cheap alternatives: a piece of hardboard (masonite), plywood or perspex (plastic) will suit just as well as long as you seal the surface. The traditional way of doing this is to rub linseed oil into the wood and repeat the process over a period of two or three days. This will prevent the surface soaking up the oil from the paint. However, a quicker way to seal the surface is to use shellac or button polish, either of which can be painted on, or rubbed in. Paper palettes are very practical when you are in a hurry; by simply tearing off the top layer of paper and disposing of it, you are left with a clean white surface for next time.

Diluents

As well as being used to clean your palette and brushes, the function of diluents is to thin or dilute the paint and help it spread over the painting surface.

It is essential that the solvent used should evaporate from the paint as it dries. Turpentine is the best solvent and there are two types: distilled turpentine (the more expensive) is pure turpentine made from pine resin and gives off a strong and distinctive although not unpleasant smell; turpentine substitute (or white spirit) is made from petroleum oils. Both can be used safely to thin paint but pure turpentine is best for painting, and white spirit is best kept for cleaning purposes.

It is worth pointing out that both sorts of turpentine have a strong smell and that some people are either allergic to turpentine products or just cannot stand the smell. To overcome this, manufacturers Pelican introduced Master Colour, a paint which has all the properties of oil paint, but it is soluble in water and is completely odourless. At present, the colour range is rather more limited than the traditional oil paints.

Mediums

The subject of mediums is a complex one for beginners. To start with, quite a number are produced. Some are very traditional mediums and binders of oil and varnishes of varying recipes, others are more modern acrylics and resins, produced by various manufacturers. Like diluents, mediums can be used to thin the paint, but they are also used to modify the paint in some way – perhaps to improve its consistency for impasto painting or to increase its drying time. Linseed oil has been the most popular medium through the ages, but other oils such as poppy are also used. However, I feel that the standard of paint manufacture today is of such a high level and consistency that unless you need a specific quality – a very glossy paint, for example, or an absence of brush marks – as a beginner, you need not concern yourself with the problem of what to use at this point. Later you can experiment with different kinds – nearly all the bottles have labels which explain the different attributes of the particular mediums. For example, pure linseed oil slows drying, and increases the gloss of the paint; poppy oil gives the paint a creamy consistency, good for *alla prima* – the method of oil painting used for the projects in this book; Wingel is good for glazing and thicker paint; and Liquin is good for glazing, gives gloss and increases the drying time.

A dipper is simply a receptacle for the painting medium and cleaning agent. They are usually made of metal and can be clipped on to the palette. Dippers are especially useful if you are painting outdoors. For cleaning brushes, it is more useful to have a jar or old tin for the cleaning agent.

Easels

There are several types of easel available to the artist: the main point to remember is that the purpose of the easel is to provide a firm and stable support to your picture while you are working, so make sure that you pick the right one for the job. The most versatile is the radial or studio easel, which are manufactured by most of the well-known art suppliers. All are made to a similar pattern, and although fairly expensive will last a lifetime. They will support your smallest picture to a work about 1.75m (6ft) high comfortably.

A light sketching easel is ideal for outside work. These are folding and can be easily carried, but obviously the size of picture they can support is limited. Sketching easels are made in either wood or metal: the metal ones are lighter but slightly more expensive.

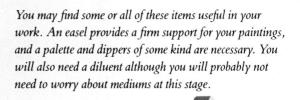

The table easel is a useful way of supporting a painting, especially if you are working in an area with limited floor space.

In the absence of an easel it is possible to use the back of an old chair as a support for a small painting.

You may find some or all of these items useful in your work. An easel provides a firm support for your paintings, and a palette and dippers of some kind are necessary. You will also need a diluent although you will probably not need to worry about mediums at this stage.

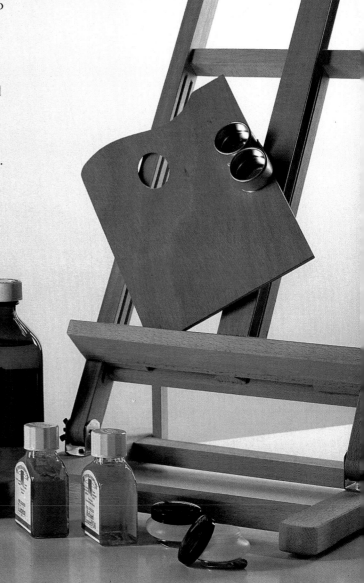

Painting supports

The painting support is the surface on to which you apply your paint. For oil painting, this has to be a non-porous surface and have sufficient tooth to hold the paint. To achieve this the surface of most supports has to be sealed. The most traditional material for painting is canvas which has been in use as a support since the fifteenth century. As well as its pleasing natural qualities of weave and texture, it has the advantage of being light and easy to carry. There are several different textures or weights of canvas available and what you decide on really does depend on the way you

Oil painting supports: (from left) smooth cartridge paper, rough cartridge paper, canvas board, Daler board, unprimed canvas, primed canvas, ready stretched canvas, strengthened hardboard and muslin.

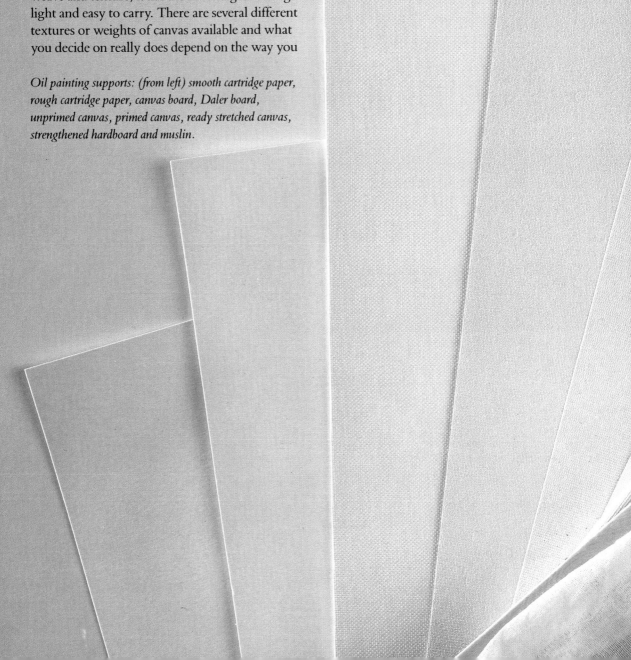

prefer to work. If you paint thinly and with a great deal of detail, then you will find that a smooth-grain canvas will suit you best. On the other hand, a heavier coarse grain will be better for the thicker impasto way of working. All art suppliers sell ready prepared canvases in a variety of shapes and sizes but you will find that they are expensive. A much cheaper way of working with canvas is to buy the canvas by the metre or yard and stretch and prepare it yourself. Stretching the canvas is not difficult. The wooden stretcher pieces you will need are available either at the art suppliers or canvas stockists.

When you buy your canvas you will find that you have a wide choice. The best quality and therefore most expensive is linen canvas, easily recognizable by its darker brown colour. A cheaper version is cotton canvas which is also available in various textures and weights and is generally the most popular. You will notice that it is also much whiter than linen canvas.

Priming a canvas

Having stretched it, you are ready to prime the canvas. The purpose of priming is to separate the painting from the canvas – if the paint is applied to the raw canvas it will soak into the fibres of the material and eventually rot them. It will also have an effect on the look of the painting: paint used in this way has a dull, rather dry look. There are many examples of modern paintings which have been carried out in this way because this quality has been deliberately looked for, and the artist has stained the raw canvas. This will no doubt pose some interesting problems for future picture restorers and conservationists.

Sealing the surface is the first task, this is done with glue size (coating). Rabbit skin size is the finest and tends to be more flexible than other sizes, but really most commercial glue size will do the job. Two coats should be applied to the canvas, the first of which should be well brushed in; ideally a day should be left between each coat.

STRETCHING A CANVAS

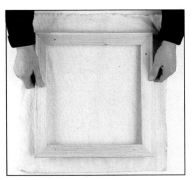

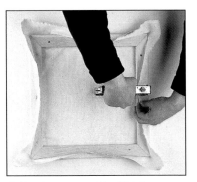

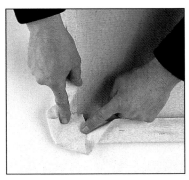

1 Lay the stretcher frame on a flat surface on top of the canvas. Mark off the amount of canvas you require, allowing a minimum of 5cm (2in.) overlap on all four sides. Remove the stretcher and cut the canvas parallel to the weave. Replace the stretcher on top of the canvas, making sure all the angles of the frame are square.

2 Starting on one side, fold the canvas over the stretcher and tack it with a staple gun in the centre. Pull the canvas taut and repeat this on the opposite side, then do the two remaining sides. Continue round the stretcher in this way, always working on opposite sides, and from the centre to the corners.

3 When you come to the corners, pull the corner of the canvas over, keeping it taut.

The next stage is to apply the ground. This will be the surface for your painting and will also serve as a further protection for the support. The ground should be an oil-based one which when dry should remain flexible to prevent the surface from cracking. There are many ready prepared grounds which can be purchased in artists' materials shops. They are always white, and at least two coats should be applied, but again this will depend on personal preferences as to the quality of surface you wish to achieve.

Another, quicker, method of preparing the canvas is to use acrylic primer which is water based and should be applied directly to the canvas without the glue size. This requires three or four coats, the first of which should be thinner and thoroughly brushed into the canvas. Priming in this way results in a good flexible ground which will take oil paint or acrylic paints equally well.

It is also possible to buy newly primed canvas by the metre or yard; this is fairly expensive but is still a good deal cheaper than buying ready stretched canvases.

The most commonly used support apart from canvas is hardboard (masonite). This is a much cheaper alternative and has the advantage of strength – it will take more knocks than canvas. It is, however, far heavier and a larger size will need wooden supports to prevent it bending and warping. Hardboard still has to be sealed and given a ground in the same way as canvas. The most popular method is to use acrylic primer or plain white emulsion (latex) paint which eliminates the need for glue size and is cheaper by far. The finished surface is, obviously, hard and smooth, unlike canvas.

Never use the rough side of the hardboard to paint on, for although it superficially has the appearance of canvas, it is entirely unsuitable, due to its unsympathetic mechanical surface. It is almost impossible to get rid of paint if you do paint on it. If you do want a canvas type of

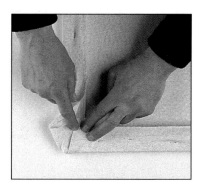

4 Fold one section of the canvas neatly into the frame, then fold the other section over it.

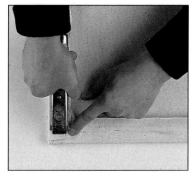

5 Staple through all the layers. It is important not to pull the canvas too tight, it should be taut and smooth. If it is too tight when you prime it the shrinkage caused by the priming will warp the shape and if really tight can split the canvas.

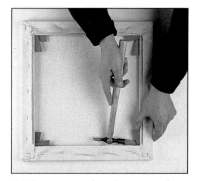

6 When you purchased your stretcher pieces you should have been given eight little wedges, two for each corner. These should be gently pushed into the slots on the inside of the corners. They enable you to tighten the canvas if it should slacken off due to atmospheric changes in the course of painting.

COVERING HARDBOARD

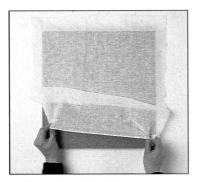

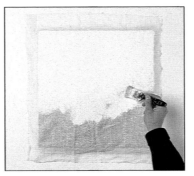

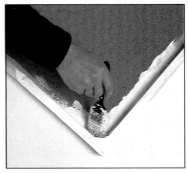

1 Cut a piece of muslin approximately 5cm (2in.) larger all round than the piece of hardboard you intend to use.

2 Glue the muslin to the shiny side of the hardboard with acrylic or emulsion primer. Brush through the fabric.

3 Turn the board over and glue the muslin to the hardboard supports. Make sure you glue well into the corners.

surface, muslin can be attached to the hardboard. Use the acrylic or emulsion primer to glue the muslin to the hardboard, making sure that you leave enough material (about 5cm/2in.) to turn over round the edges. This will need several coats of priming but will produce an interesting surface at low cost.

There are other ready prepared supports available in the form of oil painting papers, some bound like sketchbooks, and canvas boards or Daler boards which have a canvas-like surface. These are fairly inexpensive, and readily available. Lastly, plain heavy cartridge (drawing) paper and card can be used for oil painting if you treat the surface with emulsion paint before you start. This will provide a good working surface for quick sketches out of doors or in the studio.

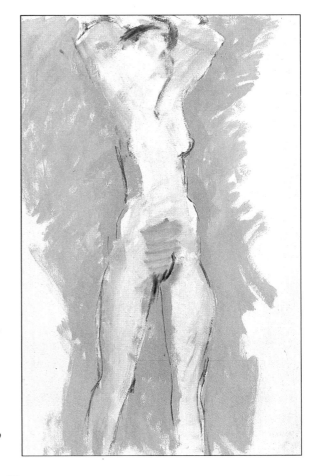

This is an example of oil paint used on cartridge (drawing) paper. It was a quick study, and the paint was kept thin, almost like a wash of watercolour except that, by using oil paint, the study has the vibrancy and strength needed without having to rely on the whiteness of the paper as one would with watercolour. It will also remain wet enough to work in for the duration of the drawing. Charcoal is used to define direction and shape.

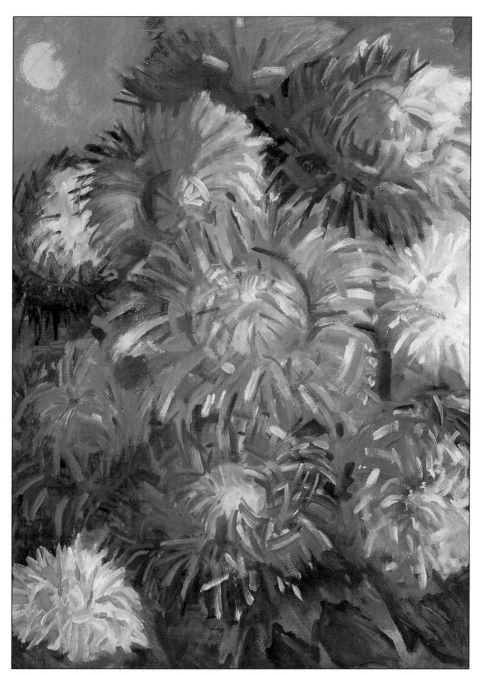

Cheryl Gould 'Flowers' 770 × 550mm (30 × 21½in.). This painting was carried out on a heavy watercolour paper. This forms a tough surface and also has a pleasing texture which holds brush marks well. The paint has been applied in a wide range of ways, from thin staining in places, building up to thick impasto. Flowers provide a good range of colours and tones, and although each flower shape is composed of small petal shapes, great care has been taken to ensure that the overall form of flowers is not lost.

Recommended kit

In order to complete the exercises and projects in this book, you will need:

Paints For the exercises and first project you will need the following oil colours: yellow ochre, raw sienna, raw umber, burnt umber (these can be Students' colours), alizarin crimson, cadmium red, cadmium yellow, cobalt blue, viridian green and flake white. For the second project you would probably need in addition light red, magenta, geranium rose, cadmium orange, lemon yellow, terre verte, cerulean blue, ultramarine, mauve, indian red and black.

Brushes Initially, you should have four bristle brushes – a No. 10 filbert and No. 10 flat, No. 6 round, and a No. 4 filbert – and one 'soft' brush for drawing in. A No. 3 mix of sable and ox or soft nylon is probably most suitable.

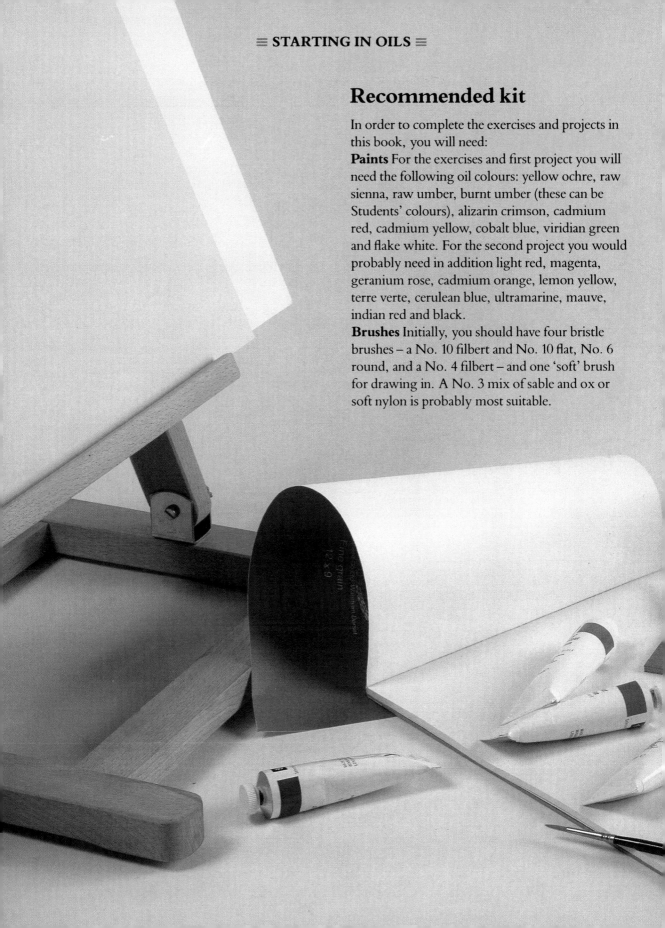

Knives A flat palette knife will be adequate for the first project, and a trowel type for the second. Either is suitable for the exercises.

Supports A pad of oil-sketching or painting paper (canvasette) is adequate for the exercises. For the first project, a Daler board is probably the most suitable support; for the second, hardboard (masonite) or canvas board, or the largest size Daler board available (60 × 72cm/25 × 30in.), may be more appropriate.

Additional items An easel, either sketching or table, or failing that use the back of an old chair; a palette, either a ready-made wooden one, or one from glass, hardboard, plastic or paper, the important thing is to have a clean surface on which to lay out and mix your paints; rags for wiping; and a dipper or jar for turpentine.

A beginner's basic oil-painting kit.

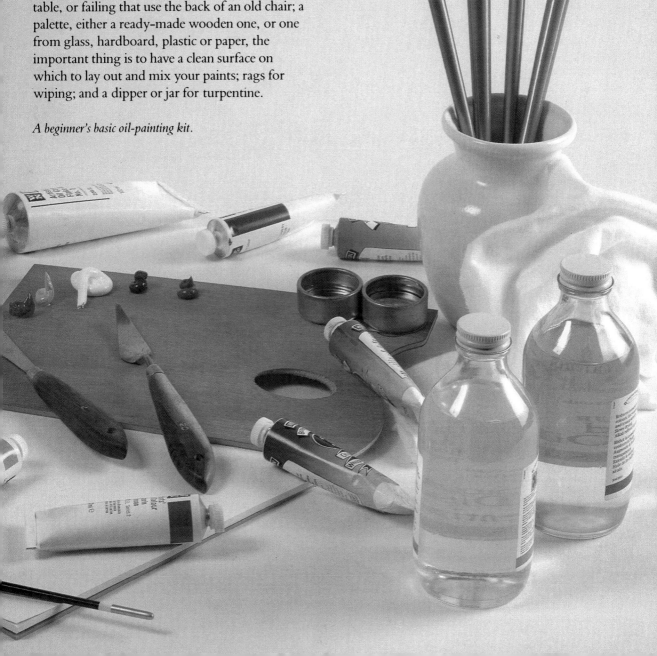

Starting to paint

The list of materials given on pages 22-3 is fairly comprehensive and eventually you will certainly need most, if not all, of them. At the beginning, however, this is not necessary. The first really important thing to do in oil painting is to get the feel of the paint and enjoy the qualities that are specific to oil paint, and explore the range of marks you can make with your various brushes. The idea of carrying out exercises before you make a proper painting is rather like doing finger exercises in music, limbering up without having the complication of trying to paint objects or a landscape.

At this stage, I would suggest a series of small exercises (say 15 × 15cm/6 × 6in.) exploring the qualities of the paint and surface. You may wish to expand on these and develop them in further exercises of your own.

> **You will need**
> ▦ paints
> ▦ brushes
> ▦ painting knife
> ▦ a pad of oil-sketching paper or some Daler boards
> ▦ a palette
> ▦ a dipper containing turpentine
> ▦ rags

Use of brushes

Explore the range of marks that your brushes are capable of: this can either be in the form of a random doodle or a more organized chart which you can refer back to – it is really a matter of personal choice. The main object is to familiarize yourself with various brush marks. This will soon give you the confidence to select an appropriate brush for a particular task when you are working on a painting and will help you to enlarge your range of techniques.

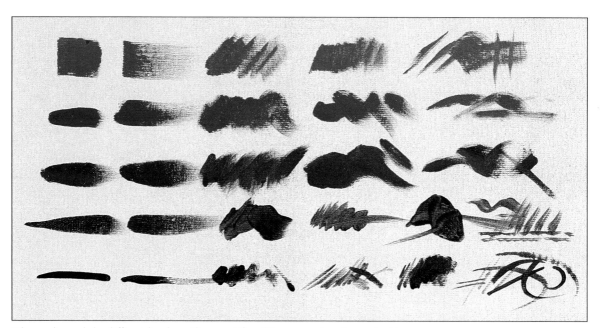

The marks made by different brushes: (from top) flat, filbert, round, nylon and sable.

Laying out your palette

Obviously the way you lay out your palette is a matter of personal preference, but to enable you to work with more speed and fluency, it is advisable to establish an order for the colours on the palette, and stick to it. This will ensure that you can find them without having to spend time looking for them. The two small palettes illustrated here are laid out from warm to cool, with white as the divider, then the earth colours. One alternative would be to lay the colours out from light to dark, with white first, then moving through the colour range, as shown in the photograph of my palette.

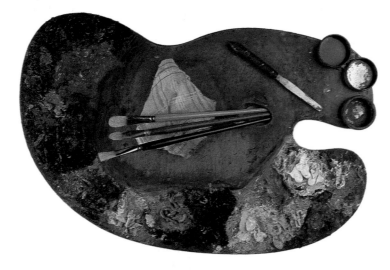

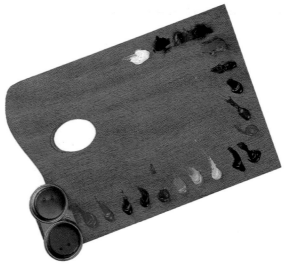

My palette: white, raw sienna, naples yellow, cadmium yellow, lemon yellow, chrome yellow, cadmium orange, viridian, terre verte, emerald green, cinnabar green, chrome green, cerulean blue, alizarin crimson, magenta, cobalt violet, cadmium red, bright red, cobalt blue, ultramarine, black.

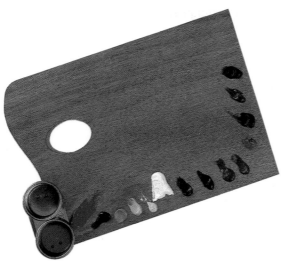

From warm to cool, with white as the divider, and earth colours to one side: cadmium red, alizarin crimson, cadmium orange, cadmium yellow, lemon yellow, flake white, viridian, ultramarine, cobalt blue, violet, yellow ochre, burnt umber, indian red, black.

Again from warm to cool, an extended palette: cadmium red, light red, crimson, magenta, geranium rose, cadmium orange, cadmium yellow, lemon yellow, viridian, terre verte, cerulean blue, cobalt blue, ultramarine, mauve, yellow ochre, burnt umber, indian red, black, flake white.

Colour

Although, at this stage, it is not necessary to go too deeply into colour theory, it is useful for the beginner to know about warm and cool colours. The phrase is used a great deal by artists when describing techniques or talking about the use of colour in a painting. The best place to start is with the colour wheel, a man-made device used to illustrate and explain colour theory. It is rather like a chart based on the colour spectrum found by passing light through a prism, but the important point to remember is that the artist is dealing with pigments which derive their colour through reflected, rather than direct, light.

The colour wheel illustrated is based on pigments. It was devised by Johannes Itten, who taught colour theory and practice to artists at the Bauhaus, in the 1930s. It starts with the three primary colours – red, yellow, and blue. These are pure colour and cannot be made by mixing together other pigments, but they do form the basis of the rest of the colour wheel. Surrounding these primaries are the secondary colours, which are a mixture of the primaries – red and yellow

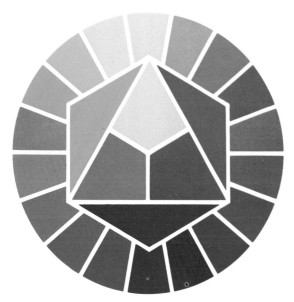

The colour wheel.

produce orange, yellow and blue produce green, and red and blue give violet. The colours of the outer circle are known as tertiary colours. These are mixtures of the primary and secondary colours which give different strengths of colour. Red and orange, for example, will produce a red-orange, due to the predominance of the primary red in the two colours when mixed. Yellow and orange will produce a yellow-orange, and so on.

If the circle is divided in half, two groups of colour are formed – cool colours and warm colours. That is to say the colours of one half are warm in feeling compared with the rest of the colours which are cool in feeling. The word feeling is very important because it is an emotional response to the colours which makes us decide that they are warm or cool, although obviously there are associations within the range – reds, yellows and oranges make us think of fire, sun, heat, and so on, while in the cool range blues, greens and blue-violets make us think of sky, water and ice. This way of looking at colour is used extensively in the advertising industry where a particular mood or feeling is important.

Within the broad general terms 'warm' and 'cool', however, it is possible to find warmer and cooler variations – there are warmer greens and colder blues, and so on. A touch of red or violet in a blue will make it slightly warmer than a pure blue. These variations are infinite and very finely balanced. The degree of warmth or coolness also depends on the colours that surround a particular colour – chrome yellow placed next to lemon yellow will make the lemon yellow look cooler; viridian green next to lemon yellow will make the lemon yellow look warm.

There are examples of paintings which are predominantly warm or cool, and have been deliberately painted as such by the artists to convey a particular emotion to the spectator. In this way colour is as important as line or form in a composition. Specific use of warm or cool colours can also create a sense of space in a painting. You will notice in nature that distance tends to make colours appear cooler – they take on a blue, hazy quality, because of the way the atmosphere affects how we see the colours. You will notice, however, that even in many old landscape paintings the artists used blues and other cool colours for backgrounds to create a feeling of distance, and warmer colours in the foreground to create the feeling of nearness. The Impressionists, too, used colour theory to create the feeling of light and vibrancy in their paintings. Today, abstract painters who may be unconcerned with any figurative elements in their works will achieve the feeling of space through their manipulation of colour theory.

Colour mixing

According to the colour wheel, it should be possible to produce all the colours you need from the primaries – red, yellow and blue. Unfortunately, this is not strictly true; there are some colours it is just not possible to create and the more intense violets, purples, greens and some blues have to come from a tube.

When you choose your oil colours you will find that there are various types of red, yellow and blue. It is very important to know the differences between them. Cadmium red, for example, is very near the primary red in the colour wheel. You will find that when you mix cadmium red with cadmium yellow you can achieve a good orange, near to the orange in the colour wheel. However if you use a crimson red with the cadmium yellow, the orange goes brown and the brilliance goes from it. The same applies with the yellows. Cadmium yellow is as good a primary as you will get, and mixed with cadmium red it gives a good orange, but lemon yellow will give a dull orange lacking in brightness.

These differences run through to the blues when mixed with reds. Our primary red (the cadmium), when mixed with cobalt blue, according to the colour circle should give us a good violet, but it will in fact make brown. To achieve violet, mix crimson red with blue.

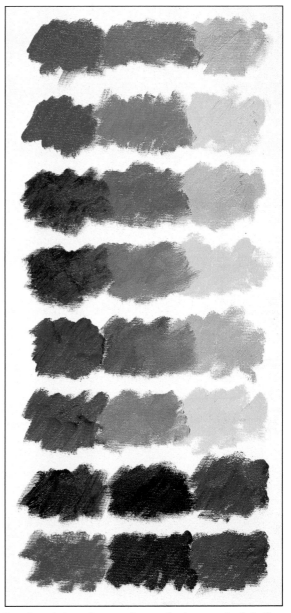

Practise mixing colours so that you begin to get the feel of how the various pigments will react together and the colours you can make: (from top) cadmium red + cadmium yellow (this is a 'true' orange); cadmium red + lemon yellow; crimson red + cadmium yellow; crimson red + lemon yellow; cobalt blue + cadmium yellow (the 'truest' green); cobalt blue + lemon yellow; crimson red + cobalt blue (a 'true' violet); and cadmium red + cobalt blue.

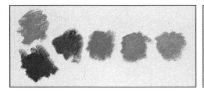 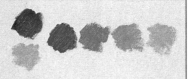 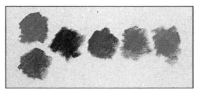

Mixing primary and secondary complementaries plus increasing amounts of white. Orange and cobalt blue make a cool grey, violet and cadmium yellow, and green and cadmium red make warm greys, almost flesh tints.

It is useful at this stage to try small mixes of these colours and note the different results for future reference. The more you play with your paints and become familiar with the way they behave, the quicker you build up a knowledge which will become second nature as you work.

Wet into wet

There are many examples of the use of this technique, most often by abstract painters. It is an exciting way to explore the qualities, properties and possibilities of oil paint.

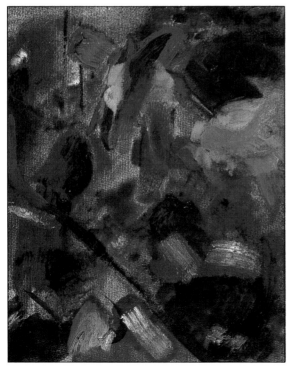

Wet into wet, thick paint worked into thin.

Mix a small quantity of thin paint to the consistency of watercolour. Then lay it on the surface quite freely. While this is still wet, add some thicker paint, of another colour, into the wet surface, perhaps scrubbing it around with a brush in some areas.

You will notice that the colour tends to bleed into the wet background, giving soft fuzzy edges in the areas where it is thinnest. Where it is slightly thicker, it will sit on top of the surface. You can also see how the colours will intermix on the surface in varying degrees of intensity.

Overall, this method gives a soft, translucent quality to the shapes, and a magical atmosphere and almost dreamlike aspect to the paint. In the areas where the paint is thicker, it seems to have a depth to it.

Glazing

Glazing is a very useful technique in many ways. It will give parts of a painting a rich glowing effect, and can also be used to overpaint and unify areas without having to repaint them totally.

Prepare an area of solid random shapes and let them dry off – this should take about 24 hours. When the paint is dry, overlay thin transparent paint of different colours. Use a soft brush for this so that you avoid any brush marks. The thinness of the overpainting will allow the colour beneath the glazed paint to show through, and it is this that gives the glowing effect to the painting.

You will notice that the colours have a brilliance which can only be achieved in this way. A green which is painted over a more solid area of green and blue, for example, intensifies in richness;

GLAZING

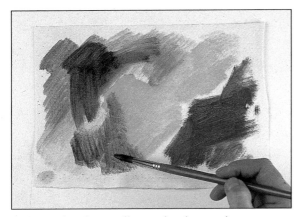

1 Green glazed over yellow tends to become sharper and brighter.

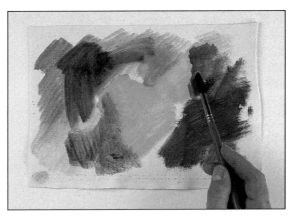

2 Blue over yellow. The colours mix on the surface, not on the palette.

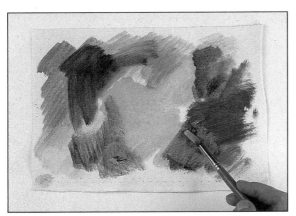

3 Yellow over blue; yellow over darker colours often appears more solid.

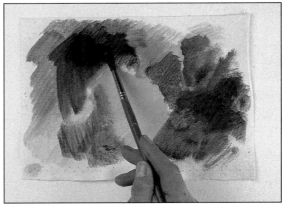

4 Areas of purple glazed over other colours enhance the feeling of space.

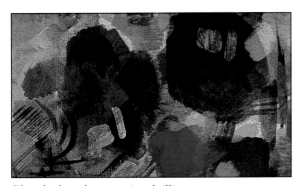

Glazed colours have a unique brilliance.

painted over bright yellow, it becomes sharper and brighter. This is also true of the reds and blues.

The colours used for the solid shapes in this example have been thinned down and overlaid across each other. It is interesting to note that some colours, like the yellow, when painted over darker shapes, actually appear more solid – this can be seen, for instance, on the green and purple shapes. This overlaying can also enhance the feeling of space; even in this small exercise, the special aspect has emerged quite naturally.

Dragged brush techniques

In this exercise, keep the paint fairly thick and stiff in consistency. Start by dragging the brush strokes across the surface, noticing the texture made by the brush and surface together. Also, mix the brush marks together, enjoying the feeling of fluidity of the thick wet paint.

While this is drying, drag some more paint over the surface of the brush marks. You will find that the wet paint will move uncontrollably. This effect can be used consciously in your paintings.

You will also notice that the paint sticks to the raised texture and gives a gritty or dry feeling. It can also add a sparkle to the surface, and gives a completely different effect from the previous exercise. This sparkle can be very useful in the finishing stages of a painting.

Using a painting knife

Many people find thick paint more exciting to work with than thin, and the element of chance involved in knife painting – it is not so controllable as a brush mark – is in itself stimulating to many artists.

There are many ways to use a painting knife. The paint can be laid on to the surface very thickly to lose the surface texture of the ground

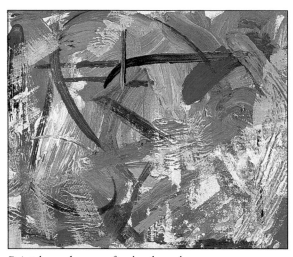

Paint dragged over surface brush marks.

completely. Alternatively, it can be lightly scraped or dragged over the surface to create a broken, sparkling feeling. It can also be used in conjunction with a brush. The contrast of marks adds extra interest.

The colour lies on the surface of the canvas or board in a different way from paint that is brushed on and there are no brush marks. The paint also usually has sharper edges than you could achieve with a brush.

There are many examples of well-known artists who have made extensive use of the knife in their paintings; a notable example is John Constable.

KNIFE PAINTING

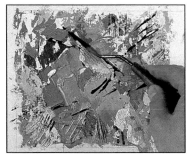

1 Using the edge of the knife will give a sharp linear mark.

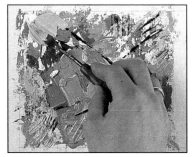

2 Using the whole blade flat allows a full gestural movement.

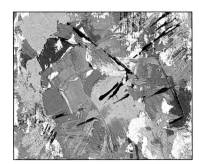

3 Knife painting gives a surface free from brush marks.

SCUMBLING

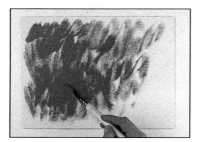

A colour scumbled over the support will mean areas of the white ground will show through.

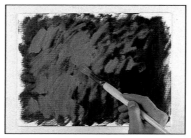

Scumbling light over dark, the previous colour is still visible and changes the lighter colour.

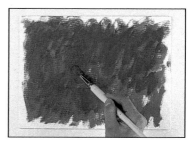

Dark over light – the eye tends to mix the colours on the surface of the painting.

Scumbling

Scumbling is applying thick paint loosely and freely over the surface of a painting. It can be used to add interest to large plain areas of work, it can also give a glowing effect to the surface, tone down passages of a painting, produce a softness in places, and can add freshness and light.

Scumbling can be used on a surface that is already painted, or applied over an untinted ground. The colour underneath the scumble will show through. This gives an exciting broken, dappled effect. Different effects can be achieved, according to whether the scumble is lighter or darker than the ground. Also, depending on the colours you use, laying broken colours over one another can mean that the eye will mix the colours on the surface of the painting.

You can achieve interesting effects by scumbling the paint on with a rag or tissue, rather than a brush. This can give a variety of textures and effects to the surface of the painting.

The doodle

The doodle incorporates all or most of the elements in the smaller single exercises. The advantage of it is that the elements all interact and the various qualities complement each other. The only organization I allowed myself was that on one side the colour is thin and transparent in feeling, and on the other side the paint is thick and gestural with more intermixing of the colours and white so that you notice the subtle tonal variation. What is also interesting in this doodle is the quality of the thin transparent paints. They seem to float and create space and distance of a different kind from the thicker areas.

The way to learn from this exercise and also the smaller ones is to stop and really examine what you have done. At this stage, there will be a good many accidental qualities which are sometimes quite magical and can be used and made to work for you in a more considered situation later on.

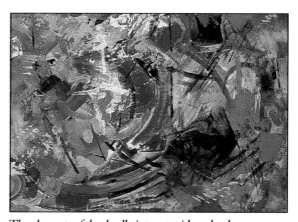

The elements of the doodle interact with each other.

31

Project: A still life 1

The simple still-life group is an excellent way for the newcomer to oil painting to experiment and learn about the medium. By working indoors, you don't have all the problems encountered outside, such as changing light, and unwanted spectators. At this stage, it is more important to learn to manipulate the paint and experiment with different brushes and ways of applying the paint. It is only by doing this that you find the ways that suit you best and develop your own technique, which eventually becomes as personal and unique as handwriting. For this painting, I will show how to build from thin paint to thick in one sitting. By keeping the first areas thinly painted, the surface remains in a good state to make alterations and adjustments.

You will need
- paints
- brushes
- painting knife
- a Daler board, about 40 × 50cm (16 × 20in.)
- a palette
- a dipper containing turpentine
- rags
- a pencil and cartridge paper, for sketches

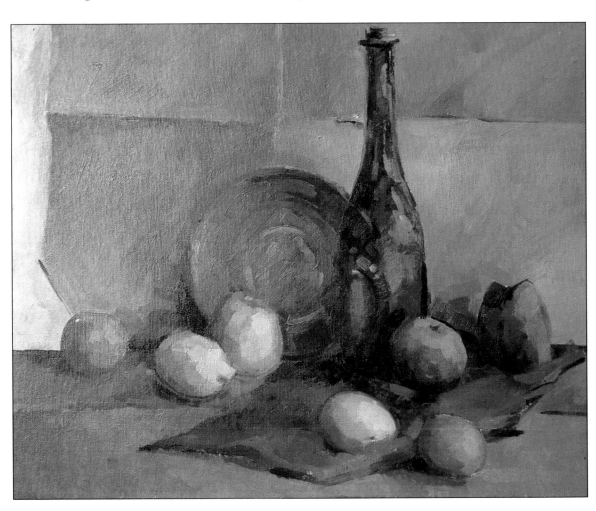

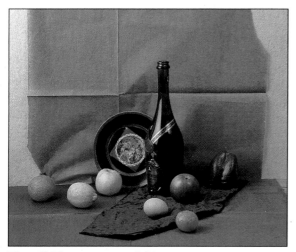

The still-life arrangement of objects.

Choice of subject

For this first project, I have set up a very simple still life using objects that are easily found around the home. Coloured paper creates areas of tone and colour in the simplest possible way. This avoids the complexities of folds and texture which you will find with drapery.

I have used the fruit and the plate because of their simplicity of shape. All are almost round, but have the variation and subtlety of colour needed to help you to see the changes of colour and tone in an individual object. You will also notice here that there is a relationship of colour which connects the objects and background throughout the picture. The predominant colour is established by the green background. The colour then ranges through a variety of greens in the apples and bottle, working its way through to the palest apple which is almost yellow to the full yellow of the lemon. Then, from the yellow of the lemon it is a natural step to the yellow-orange and full orange of the oranges themselves which intensify into the reds of the red apple. The blue of the small piece of drapery seems to act as an accent due to its opposition to the orange colour. I used the egg because of its simple smooth shape which when placed on the blue seemed to pick up the blues and grey-pinks of the colours around it.

Preliminary sketches

The viewpoint I have chosen is a flat and straight on view. This means that there are almost no perspective problems. It is a good idea before you start to make one or two very simple sketches just to get the composition right. As you will see from the first little drawing that I made, the composition was not satisfactory. The bottle and plate were practically central to the picture, thus creating a rather obvious viewpoint, but moving this focus over to the right of centre and adding the light strip to the left-hand side achieves a better balance and more interest. This will only take a few minutes of your time but it is invaluable when planning your picture.

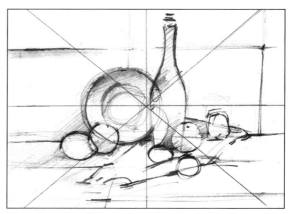

Here, the point of interest is much too central.

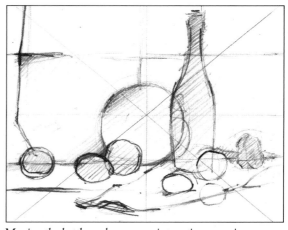

Moving the bottle makes a more interesting grouping.

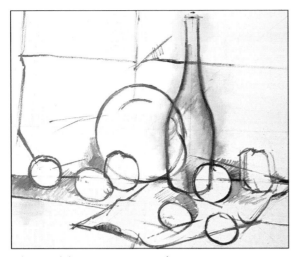

The initial drawing in in raw umber.

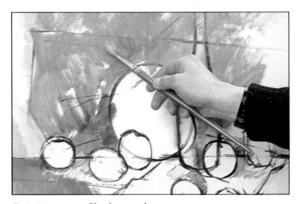

Painting areas of background.

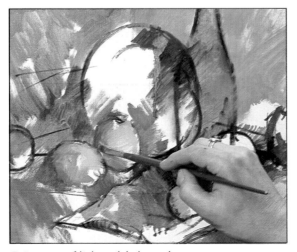

Paint areas of light and dark together.

When sketching in your composition on your board, use the minimum amount of drawing. Remember that almost all of the drawing will eventually be covered up. You only need to indicate, as accurately as possible, the sizes and shapes of the objects and their relationship to each other. Draw with sable using a neutral colour, in this case I used raw umber. The first drawn lines can be sketched in in pencil before the paint is used. Charcoal is sometimes used, but it tends to mix in with the first application of paint, which could present problems for the beginner.

I arranged my group of objects so that the light source comes into the picture from the side; this enhances the dramatic effect of light and dark and, more importantly for the beginner, it simplifies the way we see the forms. You will find that when you come to paint out of doors, the light source can present difficult handling problems (see pages 49-50), particularly if you work on a single painting all day, as the light is constantly changing. It requires a good deal of skill to organize the pace and tone of the picture right from the start to take this into account.

Painting the background

The second stage of the painting is to paint in thinly and in a general way the broad areas of colour and tone, letting the drawing show through. Don't worry about the colours overlapping, and don't try to paint each object separately – remember that it is the whole of the painting that you are concerned with. Use fairly large brushes so that you keep the surface free in feeling. This will also stop you fiddling with small details at this early stage.

I started with the background first only because it is the largest single area, but once a general statement was made, I quickly moved on to the smaller areas. It is important to try and paint these together, by that I mean if you are painting one area of the plate, you will look and make a decision regarding the colour and tone of a corresponding area next to it, which might be the bottle or background. In this way, the whole painting will gradually build up and you will avoid painting objects singularly. Paint lights and darks together, this will help you to make judgements as to the relative value of light and dark. You will also notice that although there are colour changes, as in the green pepper next to the blue drapery, the tones at their darkest are about the same. This is also true of the oranges and apples and the corresponding backgrounds. This is an important point to learn. While colours may change, tones may well come together. This is what will give a painting atmosphere and will get away from the feeling that the objects exist completely separately.

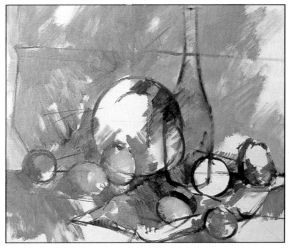

Initial areas of colour scrubbed in.

Re-establishing the drawing

You will probably find at this stage that some of the drawing has either got lost (because you have painted over it) or gone wrong in the painting. Don't worry about this – it happens in the course of a painting. All it means is that at this stage it is a good idea to re-establish the drawing in those areas where you feel it needs it. I found in this painting that it was necessary to re-draw the bottle and refine its shape, which had become clumsy. The fruit was also generally too round and was beginning to lose its character. I was able to change these without difficulty because I had kept the paint loose and thin, and like this it is easily overpainted.

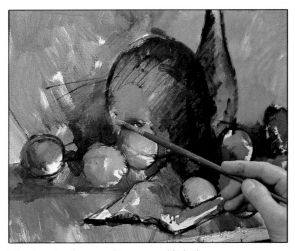

The drawing has now been re-established.

The first details

By this stage, I am being more specific and looking in more detail at shapes and the small colour changes within the objects, paying particular attention to the way the colours reflect the different colours around them. You can see that I have carried some of the warmth of the orange on the left of the lemon into the lemon itself, so that a part of the lemon is almost orange. The orange also reflects down on to the surface of the table, giving off a warmer half-tone around it. The lemon was a particularly good choice for this

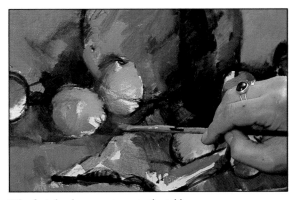

The fruit lends warm tones to the table.

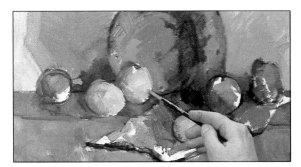

Thicker paint is used in the lighter areas.

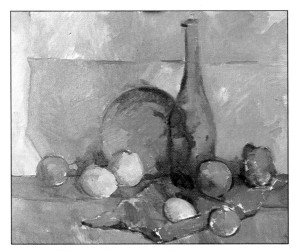

Almost all the board is now covered.

project because as you will see it seems to pick up a great deal of the colour around it – greens, oranges and browns.

I am now able to use thicker paint, particularly in the light areas. The heavier paint strokes seem to give a feeling of surfaces reflecting light while the thin dark areas give a feeling of shadow.

I have kept the paint thinner on the bottle to give more of the feeling of transparency of glass and only where the light is reflected have I allowed the paint to become thicker. In this last stage, I have defined some of the lines of the composition more fully. For example, the folds on the green background paper are important directional lines and the light shape of the wall is crucial to the balance of the composition, particularly where the light meets the dark of the table and orange. This

creates an accent and seems to balance the picture more satisfactorily. I have also found that the brightness of the orange at that point is useful in bringing the eye over to that side of the painting.

Adding the highlights

It is at this final stage that I have started to look at the highlights or lightest parts of the objects. I have carefully avoided adding these until now since they require a good deal of thought and restraint. You will find that there is a great temptation to over-emphasize the highlights and add flecks of white all over the place. When this occurs in a picture, these highlights usually look as though they are on the surface of the painting rather than on the objects themselves; in other words, they look totally unrelated to the whole.

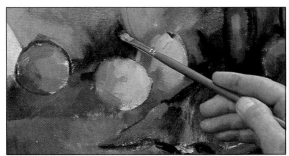

Being more specific about edges.

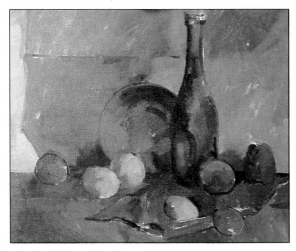

Beginning to look at the lightest areas.

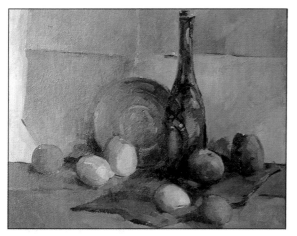

Building up the highlights.

Try to see highlights as areas of lightness of colour rather than as white reflections. I have noticed by now that the lightest points in the picture are the lemon, part of the apple next to it, the strip down the left-hand side, and the egg. All the other tones gradually come closer together so that the picture is predominantly dark and half-tones. This gives a bit of drama to the objects but, more importantly, if you can learn to look at your painting in this way, trying to sum up its whole feeling, stage by stage, you will find that you will begin to do this before you actually start painting. You will begin to apply this same sort of looking to the objects themselves.

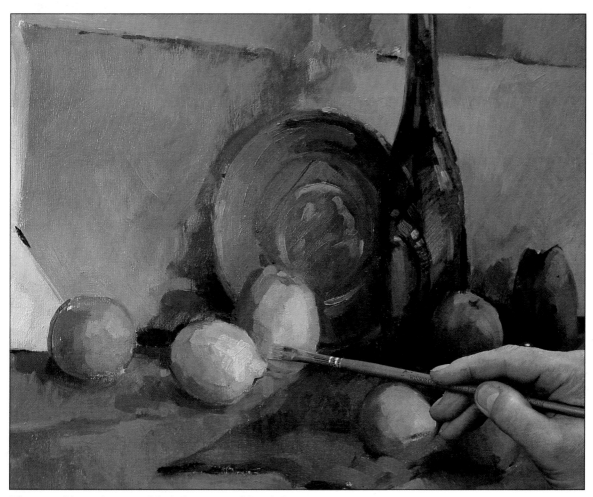

This part of the apple is one of the lightest areas of the whole painting.

Underpainting

In all the little exercises that you carried out, and in the first project, you will have noticed that the paint has stayed wet for a considerable length of time, probably all day. This is one of the basic qualities of oil paint, which gives it the advantage over water-based pigments of being flexible for change and alteration over a long period. There are two basic methods of working in oils. The first, which is the approach taken in the first project, is called *alla prima*. This simply means working the paint directly on to the canvas into wet paint. The colour is mixed on the canvas as well as on the palette. This way of working is the most usual when you are doing a painting at one sitting – a landscape, for instance – when you can only spend a short time working, or a portrait where your time is limited to a day or part of a day. The second method is a more considered approach in that you have to have decided on the relative tones of the areas of the canvas or board before you start to paint. This is a very structured approach to picture-making and requires a good deal of time and a strong idea of how the paint will look to be successful.

> **You will need**
> ☐ paints
> ☐ brushes
> ☐ oil-sketching paper or a Daler board
> ☐ a palette
> ☐ a dipper containing turpentine
> ☐ rags

Ken Howard 'Homage to Sir William Orpen' 1500 × 1350mm (60 × 50in.). This picture is a beautiful example of underpainting cool greys and whites with a warm colour. You can see the full orange on the vertical edges of the picture. The colour filters through giving a vibrancy to the cool areas and cleverly lead us to the warm tones of the head and hands.

Underpainting technique

This approach to oil painting has a strong tradition. The picture is usually begun with a more detailed drawing than in *alla prima* painting on the canvas, and is then built up in a variety of ways. Sometimes strong glazes are laid on top of the drawing and when they are dry, they are worked into with thicker paint, and perhaps over-glazed again.

The whole of this method can be carried out on the white ground, although some artists prefer to stain the ground with a colour to give extra vibrancy to the colours applied later. The colour chosen to stain the surface ground can either set the mood of the picture from the start (either warm or cool), or act as a contrast to the colours added as the painting continues.

Thinned oil paint is usually used for underpainting, although some artists use acrylics, which dry quickly.

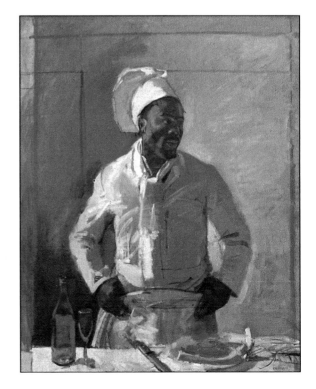

Monochrome underpainting

There is a further way of starting a painting, called underpainting in monochrome (monochrome meaning one colour). The reason for underpainting in this way is broadly to create the light and dark areas and build up the three-dimensional aspect of your picture before using colour. It is best to use a neutral colour (in the example illustrated here I used burnt umber and blue), since these have the advantage of drying quickly. Don't add white but thin the pigment down with turpentine, almost to the consistency of watercolour. For the areas you wish to be light in the finished painting, leave the ground white, and build up the layers of pigment for the darkest areas of your painting. In this way you will create the light and dark tonal areas.

UNDERPAINTING IN MONOCHROME

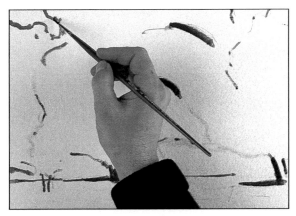

1 Drawing in the main lines and directions using burnt umber, or raw umber. Remember to keep the drawing as simple as possible.

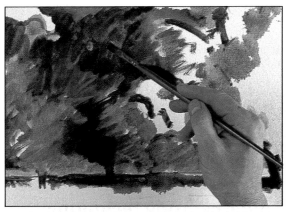

2 The next stage is to lay in quickly a thin wash of paint to indicate the feeling of shape and tone.

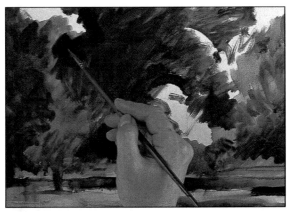

3 Here, I am starting to vary the lights and darks of the trees, keeping a general feeling of shape to preserve the dramatic quality of the trees.

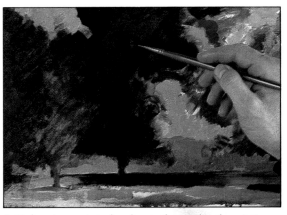

4 Colour is now introduced on to the tonal underpainting; the tone of the colour relates to the first underpainting.

Project: A still life 2

One of the outstanding advantages of painting still lifes is that you, the artist, are in complete control. You select the format, and choose and arrange the objects right from the start. You could say that it is at this point that the painting really begins. It is always a good idea to make your choice with a theme in mind. This could be the relationship of colour running through the objects and background, maybe a range of predominantly warm or cool colours. Shape could also be a strong element, for example, the linking of curved lines throughout, or the

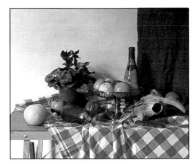

The more complex still-life arrangement for this project allows a larger format.

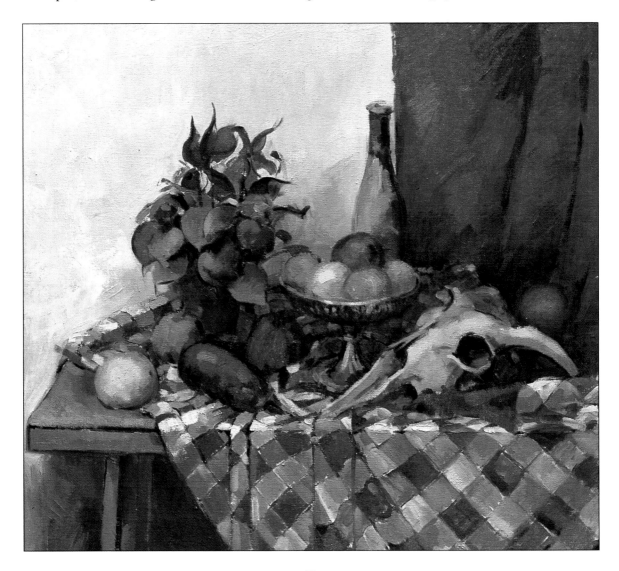

contrast of curves against straight lines, which will often produce a dramatic effect in a composition. The use of texture in a painting heightens the feeling of surfaces – this can be achieved by contrasting textural qualities within the picture, such as drapery with glass, or a piece of natural form such as bark against paper or metal. Try to avoid the idea of a picture telling a story by using objects that are only connected in the literal sense. Remember that the picture's strength lies in its composition and colour. If there is another connection, it will be secondary to these considerations. There is such a wide choice of approaches open to the artist that it is only by experimenting that you will begin to develop your own ideas about the sort of image you prefer.

> **You will need**
> ■ paints, extended colour range
> ■ brushes
> ■ trowel-type painting knife
> ■ hardboard or canvas board, 65 × 75cm (26 × 30in.)
> ■ a palette
> ■ a dipper containing turpentine
> ■ rags

Choice of objects

The format for this second still life is larger than the first, which will allow me to make a more complex grouping of objects and be more adventurous in the way the objects are arranged. Instead of flat areas of colour as in the first project, here I have used drapery, the folds of which will give me strong directional lines running through the composition. I have used fruit again because of its colour content and the way it naturally seems to relate to the colours surrounding it. The plant is an important element. Apart from being an exciting organic shape, it encompasses a great deal of the colour that occurs in the rest of the painting. Also, its overall shape and tone, seen against the light background, help to balance the strong red area on the right of the picture. The sheep's skull in the foreground is also an object which picks up all the subtle half-tones and greys of the colours around it.

I also incorporated objects with reflective surfaces – the bottle and metal fruit stand. Finally, I used the check-patterned cloth to create interest in the foreground area; this helps to give a feeling of space because of the way the checks diminish in size as they recede through the picture.

When choosing objects, try to select them from the point of view of colour and see if you can trace links of colour between them. All the objects I have chosen have these colour links, from the warm reds of the drapery and fruit through to the orange and orange-yellows of the orange and apples, then to the full yellow of the grapefruit and the green of the apples and bottle. The green of the plant is moving towards the blue of the cloth. The aubergine (eggplant) acts as a focal point of colour, because its purple quality forms a link between the blue and the red. Choice of colour is also important in creating a sense of rhythm in a composition. A good sense of rhythm means that the eye will travel through the picture from one area to another, guided by the juxtapositions between them as they overlap and cross each other. In this way, painters control how you look at their pictures, perhaps leading you gently to an important focal point.

If you consciously think in these terms when you paint, you will find that it quickly becomes second nature and it will form part of your intuitive colour sense. This applies to landscape or any other form of painting; you will see these links in almost everything in the course of everyday life, whether you are painting or not.

Choice of eye level

It is advisable for the beginner to choose an eye level either straight on or just above; in other words, if the group is set up at table height you either stand or sit to paint. If you set the group up on the floor, although visually exciting, you will create drawing problems, such as foreshortening, which at this stage are best avoided. Here, by taking a slightly higher eye level than in the first still life more of the picture surface is broken up by shape and colour.

Arranging and lighting your objects

When arranging your composition you need to consider shape, not just the shapes of the individual elements but the shape of the spaces between them. These areas are called negative shapes. They are often ignored by beginners, although they are just as important as the objects themselves. If you think of the flat surface of the picture, and then think of the pattern quality of the drawing on that surface, you can realize that the negative shapes play an important part in the whole design. You will select objects for your painting for a number of reasons, one of which will probably be that they have interesting shapes, so it should follow that all the shapes created in the picture are as interesting as possible. Lighting can also help in describing the shapes and forms of your objects. The light source can heighten the dramatic effect of a picture by casting strong dark shadows. On the other hand, a strong overall light can achieve a brilliant sparkling effect, with areas of intense highlights.

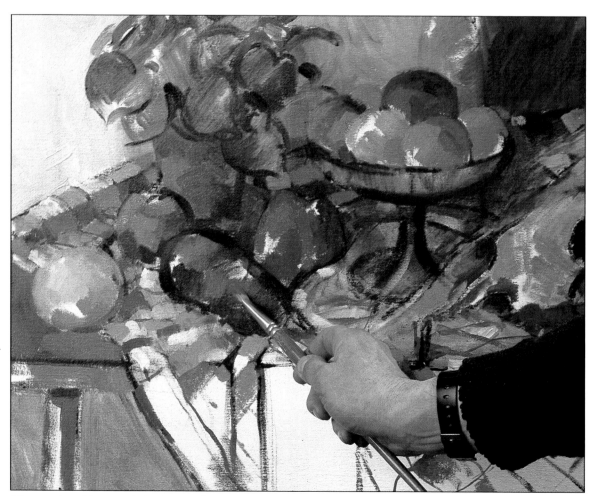

The initial scrubbing in of related areas of colour.

Initial stages

The start of the painting was the same as in the first still life, except that as the grouping was more complicated, I sketched in very lightly in pencil before making my first drawn marks in paint. This gave me more flexibility when trying to arrive at a satisfactory composition. At this stage, the painting has been kept very broad, with the paint as thin as possible, so that should I need to make changes, it will be very easy to wipe or scrape clean. You will notice that although the plant is made up of a number of elements, I have deliberately seen it as a simple overall shape and painted it loosely, rather than getting involved with the individual shapes themselves. This will come at a later stage.

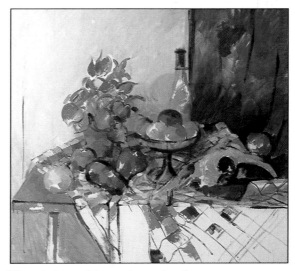

The painting at this stage is very broad.

Covering the canvas

It is also important at this early stage to try to relate the tones and colours as closely as you can, although they will almost certainly be altered and adjusted as the painting progresses. Most of the canvas is covered by now and statements of colour and tone have been made regarding all the objects and their surroundings. The only outstanding area is the checked cloth; this requires more time due to the formal nature of the pattern and needs to be drawn with some accuracy. The important thing at this stage is to establish the mood and atmosphere of the picture; this is usually through the colour and tonal relationships.

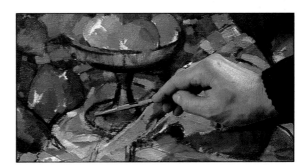

The fruit stand reflects colour around it.

The first details

By now, I am beginning to look in more detail at individual parts of the painting. The metal fruit stand as well as the area surrounding its base show how reflective surfaces provide a wide range of colours, but you must beware of and try to avoid the temptation to over-state the highlights. At this point it is more important to see how the tones are very closely related to each other and the edges almost disappear into shadow. I have also developed the other parts of the picture, notably the skull and the fruit on the stand.

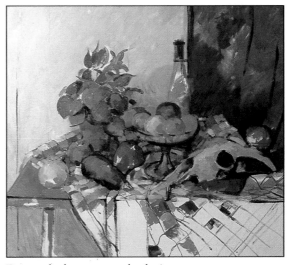

Form and colour are now developing.

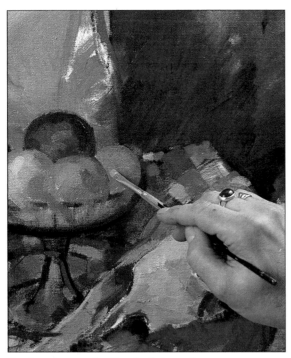

Looking in more detail at the fruit stand.

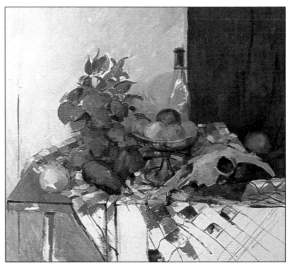

At this stage, I am more confident of colour and tone.

Colour and tonal relationships

It may be necessary at this point to re-establish the drawing in certain areas. At this stage, I am looking at the colours in the fruit stand and how they reflect into each other and change the nature of orange and yellow. You can see how the very yellow apple has taken into its shadow the orange quality of the orange fruit next to it. I am beginning to use thicker paint now, because I am confident about the colour and tonal relationships and I know that some of my marks will remain unchanged throughout the painting of the picture.

It can be seen by looking at the sheep's skull in the picture how all the subtle tones and colours seem to come together in this form. Because it is the lightest object in the group, it absorbs many of the shades surrounding it, and we can see the wonderful variety of greys which occur on the surface, warm pinky greys moving into cool green-blue greys.

Warm and cool areas

I am now working on the left-hand side of the picture. The grapefruit is an important element in the balance of the composition. The bright yellow helps to counterbalance the dark red passage in the opposite side of the picture, so the degree of

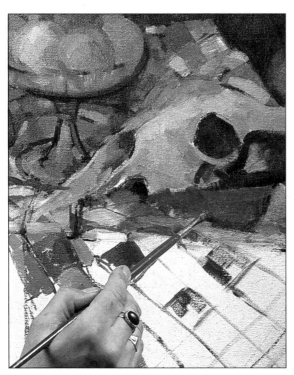

Tones and colours come together round the skull.

44

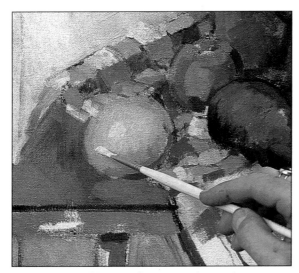

The brightness of the grapefruit is critical.

brightness is critical. If I make it too light, it will stand out too much; if I understate it, the point of it in the composition will be lost. The only immediate part of the painting which connects with it from the point of view of colour is the table top which has the same warm glow. It is also surrounded by a contrasting cool blue, so I have to relate the yellow to these colours. To do this, I notice that some of the yellow reflects down into the table top and there are areas of the yellow which take on a greeny quality which helps to bridge the gap from blue to yellow, as well as forming a link with the green apple just beyond.

At this stage, I am also beginning to paint into the checked cloth. At first sight, I am sure this complicated cloth pattern can appear daunting to the beginner, but don't be put off from using pattern in your pictures just because you feel it is too difficult. They create interesting and exciting areas in the picture, as well as being very useful in terms of composition. The best approach is to paint what you see, for instance, if you have an area of dark which is made because of the dark checks, just paint them. Don't think of them as checks, just as areas where you see definite patterns of light and dark, then it is easy to draw and paint them. If you look closely at parts of my painting you will find it hard to define precisely the check pattern, but because it is well defined in other areas, you willingly accept that the pattern runs all through the picture, even though it can't always be seen in a precise way.

Establishing the planes

At this stage, I have drawn the cloth pattern more accurately with a fine brush, and I shall now be looking closely at the way the blues change. There are basically three blues, the dark blue, lighter blue and the blue-grey. Once the formal layout has been understood, the most important aspect is how they change due to the folds and how they describe the horizontal plane of the table top and the vertical plane down the front of the table. You will notice that I am developing the front edge of the table where this change in direction takes place. The light falls mainly from above and to the side so the top plane of the table is light. I have therefore emphasized this edge by making the white checks on the top surface strong where they change direction and become darker on the vertical drop.

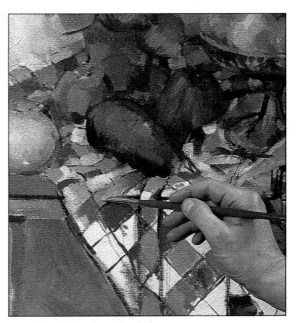

More detailed work on the cloth.

45

Balance and movement

By now I feel that it is necessary to work on the plant. This, like the grapefruit, is an important compositional element. It is important as an overall shape to balance the picture. This is achieved by the contrast in tone of dark on light and its mauve-red flowers form a link with the red drapery. This link is helped by the red of the bottle top and the red apple in the fruit stand leading the eye over to the red drapery. I am now also developing the drawing of the leaf shapes, keeping the tones close together so as not to break down the overall feeling of the plant. The sharp pointed nature of the flowers takes the eye up from the busy lower half of the picture and helps to create movement through the composition.

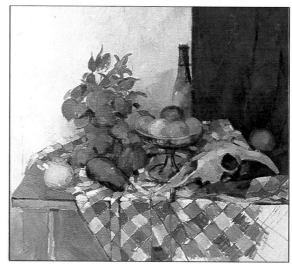

The folds of drapery are almost completed.

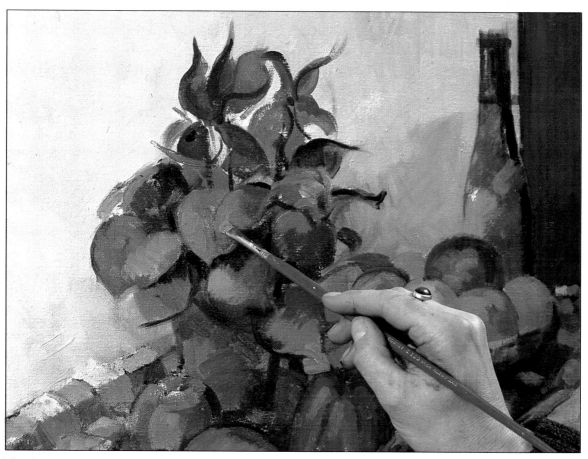

The plant is an important element in balancing the picture.

Finishing touches

As the picture is nearing completion, it is important to stop and have a good look at the whole painting so far to see if there are any parts which are not working – the drawing might need re-establishing or it might be that certain parts have become over-stated or under-stated. In my painting, at this point, I can see that the orange on the right-hand side against the red appears to be jumping forward in the picture. I could re-paint it so that it recedes, or I could try glazing it down. This is, in fact, what I have done. By glazing thin red paint over the painted orange I was able to pull it back into the drapery. I left the very centre of the orange showing through so that the edges almost disappeared. I then lightened the horn of the sheep's skull to bring it forward. It was also at this point that I painted some detail into the fruit stand and finished off the check pattern. I also felt that the table top needed lightening to give more contrast with the dark shadow underneath. This helps to bring that edge forward.

Because the light background is a large plain area I painted some of the soft tones with a palette knife to give the area a textural interest, without making it too prominent.

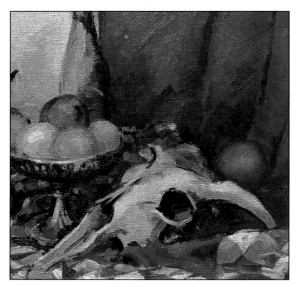

Glazing the orange pulls it back into the drapery.

Varnishing pictures

Varnishes are used for two main reasons. The first, and most important, is to protect the painted surface from damage caused by atmospheric pollution, which can cause discoloration and eventually do irreparable harm to the pigments themselves, and from minor scratches and marks. Secondly, varnishes are used to restore the original quality of colour and tone to your picture.

You will probably have noticed during the course of your work on the exercises and projects that in many cases the colour has gone dull or patchy. This is due to the way some colours dry. If they have plenty of oil ground with them they will probably stay shiny; if you have mixed a lot of turpentine with your paint it will probably have dried dull and matt. This patchy quality is irritating and distracting. To overcome it, you can use re-touching varnish. This is an ideal temporary measure and can be used straight away to restore the brilliance of the paint.

In the longer term, however, a clear picture varnish will be necessary, although you shouldn't apply this for at least nine months to a year after the picture has been completed, since it takes this amount of time for the paint to dry and harden fully. If varnish is applied before the paint is fully dry, cracking or crazing will almost certainly occur, due to the different drying times of the paint and varnish.

When you come to apply the picture varnish make sure that your painting is clean and free from dust particles. To do this, wash it gently with a soft rag or cottonwool (absorbent cotton) dipped in mild soapy water, then rinse the rag with clean water and go over the surface again to get rid of all the soap. Let it dry thoroughly. Apply the varnish with a soft varnish brush, which can be obtained from art suppliers. Start from the top and apply the varnish thinly and evenly over the whole surface at one go. If you allow one area of varnish to dry and then continue you will find that there is an edge where the two varnished layers overlap.

Subjects for the oil painter

The choice of subject for the painter is endless and what moves one person to paint a particular subject will not necessarily have the same effect on another. It is, however, a strange phenomenon about painting that someone else's interpretation of a subject which is not particularly to our liking can have the power to move us – it is not so much what you paint as how you interpret the subject. If you are drawn to a subject, do not be put off by what might seem like problems at the time, have a go. You will find that your enthusiasm will help you to surmount many of the technical difficulties, and, the more you do it, the more your technique will improve.

Oil is very suitable for many subjects for the beginner due to its flexibility. If a painting is going wrong, or proving difficult, oil will allow you to scrape or rub it off the surface and rework it again and again. The technique is obviously different from, say, watercolour, which requires a more careful and considered approach, and won't allow for much pushing around the surface. Scale also plays a part. Very large watercolours require technical know-how and time, whereas a fairly large oil painting can be tackled more readily by an enthusiastic beginner.

John Constable 'Sketch for Leaping Horses' 1294 × 1880mm (51 × 71in.). This full-size sketch shows how Constable ironed out many of the problems of composition and colour before he committed himself to the final painting. Although this is referred to as a sketch, this only means that it was a loosely painted preparatory work – it has all the completeness of a finished painting.

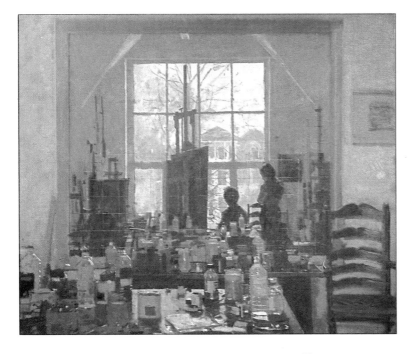

Ken Howard 'Studio Interior' 625 × 750mm (25 × 30in.). This painting of Ken Howard's is an interesting example which shows that one does not necessarily have to go far for subjects. Very often the immediate environment in which you live and work can be just as stimulating pictorially as anything which you deliberately search out.

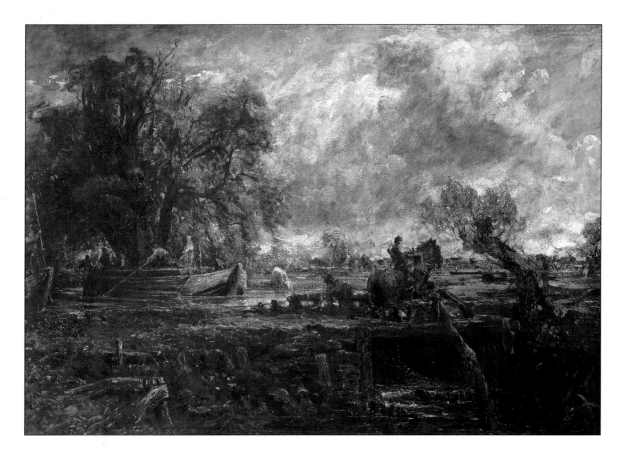

Painting out of doors

Although as we have seen, the simple still-life group is an excellent way for the newcomer to oil painting to experiment and learn about the medium, sooner or later many people (probably the majority) will feel that landscape is the subject that inspires them to want to paint most of all. So, the problems which I have outlined – light, spectators, and so on – will eventually have to be faced; the early work at home will have prepared you with the basic use of oil painting materials and the medium itself.

A clear advantage of working directly from nature is that you can compile a selection of studies of a location or subject and build them into a more considered composition. This also allows you to increase the scale to a size that would not be possible out of doors. There are many examples of this way of working. Constable made endless colour studies and drawings which he then developed into full-size sketches, then turned these into a finished painting.

The problem of light can be approached in several ways. Usually if you start painting out of doors and you intend to spend the best part of the day at it, you can assume that choosing your subject and the initial drawing will take an hour or so. During the time spent drawing and blocking in the large masses, you will not have to make major decisions about the light, except to bear in mind that it is changing very slowly. When you come to make specific decisions, save them until you are well on into the painting. Details can also be left until near the end as often the overall light won't affect how you paint them greatly.

Another way of dealing with the light is to paint on a small scale and do several paintings in a

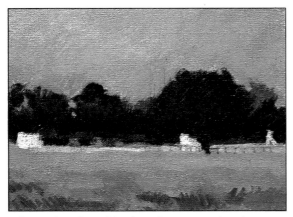

This study is formed by the rather warm sultry day making dark shadows which push the white screens in to dramatic prominence.

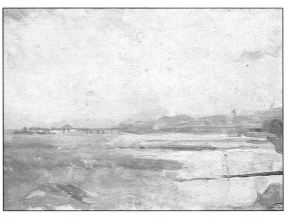

The paint in this picture varies from very thin to thicker light scumbling in the sky area to convey the light misty atmosphere of this kind of subject.

day. By doing this, you will gradually begin to catch the light and build up a series of little paintings, telling the story of the changing light over a period of time. It would then be interesting to compare how changes in light affect the feeling of the landscape over the period of a day.

If the weather is fine and sunny you will notice that the paint, especially if you put it on thinly, will dry off more quickly than indoors. This is one of the major advantages of working outside.

There are also logistical problems to working out of doors. It is advisable to keep equipment down to the absolute essentials. Make sure that the size of canvas or board is one that you can

handle – remember that you are going to be going home with a wet painting so it has to be easy to carry. Art shops sell special carrying straps for wet paintings. As for the critical spectators, well you just have to learn to live with them.

Alternatively, it is nearly always possible to paint from a window or in your garden. The window can give the picture an extra dimension, since by including it as part of the composition you convey the feeling of looking through a vista. The garden has certain advantages: you can go where you like, you can always be sure of getting the same spot again, and you can spend as much time as you wish on the painting.

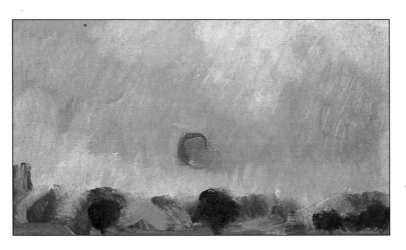

This little study was carried out on a piece of mounting card, one of many oil sketches made on the spot. Obviously it is necessary to work fast with a subject like a sunset so I have kept the scale small and the paint is very thin and washy in places.

Using photographs

You might prefer to paint portraits of people or animals, although they always pose a problem simply because they move. This is where a camera can be a useful aid. I use the word 'aid' deliberately, as there does not seem much point in taking a photograph and just reproducing in paint what was probably better as a photograph anyway! But there are times when certain information is needed, either as a supplement to a drawing, or as a way to capture quickly the feeling that you want in the picture. This, combined with quick sketches, will give added information for you to use.

Photographs can also provide the stimulus for an idea. The photograph reproduced here, for example, was taken by me on a walk in Wales. I was attracted by the colour of the moss-grown stump which was bright green, and the odd, interesting shapes of the decaying wood surrounded by spiky brambles and roots. Although I had the photograph to work from, my first impressions and memories of that encounter were more important as they formed the basis of the idea for the painting. I first made several small scribbles on paper, trying to formulate my idea. The next stage was to make a larger, more detailed drawing, working towards that precise composition. This I carried out in colour, using paint and inks. You will see that the picture has now moved away from the photograph: the basic composition has changed, and the colour is also changing. I have heightened the green of the stump and, to emphasize this, I have introduced the orange.

The photograph is now totally discarded as my drawing is to form the basis of the projected painting. I began to realize that the shapes had a sinister, almost animal-like, quality to them which was not in the photograph. This aspect I developed further in the painting. You will also see that the final painting differs from the drawing in many ways. It is not just a question of doing a

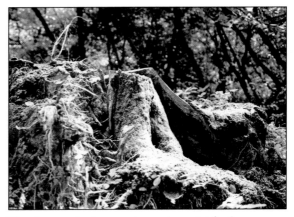

The photograph that was the starting point for the painting below.

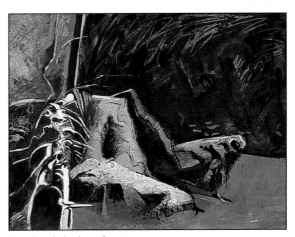

The detailed colour drawing.

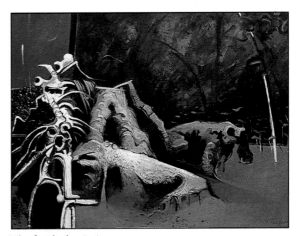

The finished painting.

painting of the drawing – there must be room for development in the painting itself. I have retained the feeling of the dark woodland but there is almost a feeling of a fantastic stage set emerging which is far from the original photograph. In this sequence I have tried to show that there are ways of working from photographs that are more than just copying them.

Painting from sketches

One of the most enjoyable and satisfying ways to acquire subjects for oil paintings is through using a sketchbook. You should never be without one, either at work or at home – think of it as a visual notebook. When you see a subject that you find interesting, jot it down. Drawings made on holiday, or on a normal day-to-day basis, will provide endless material for paintings carried out in the studio. (They will also help you to improve your drawing technique.) Obviously making the sketch studies is the first step, but when you are sketching you do not always have a finished painting in mind. So, how do you set about translating a drawing from your sketchbook into a finished painting?

Your first consideration will be to compose that initial sketch into a pleasing and well-constructed picture. You will also probably find that your first sketch is a different shape from the final format you have in mind, so you will have to alter or 'translate' your sketch to fit your new shape. The easiest way to do this is to redraw the main shapes and directions of your sketch on to another piece of paper, altering and adjusting them until you arrive at the arrangement that is most satisfying to you, and seems to work best.

The next stage is to transfer this image on to the larger shape that is to be your finished painting. For this, a system called 'gridding up' or 'squaring up' is used. This is simple to carry out. First, make sure that your small study is the same proportion as the painting is going to be. An easy method of reproducing the exact proportion from a small scale to a larger one is to lay the small shape (your drawing) on to the larger area (your painting support) tight into a corner and draw a diagonal line through the small shape, continuing it until it meets the edge of the painting support. Any rectangle drawn with that same diagonal will be in direct proportion to your smaller shape, and the area outside the point where it strikes the edge is waste. In the illustration here, any one of the coloured rectangles would be in direct proportion to the original drawing.

Having settled on the scale and proportion of your painting, you now need to transfer the drawing to the painting surface. To do this, you impose a grid structure on top of your study by drawing in two diagonals from corner to corner, then dividing it horizontally and vertically into four equal rectangles. This grid can then be subdivided as many times as you wish just by halving the shapes diagonally, horizontally and vertically. The number of times you repeat the process, obviously, depends on the complexity of the drawing you are transferring; the more detail you have the more reference points you will need. You will probably find it helps to number the grid lines.

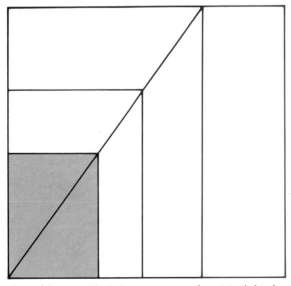

Any of the rectangles is in proportion to the original sketch.

The final step is to repeat this grid-making process on your painting support. You will now have a series of grid lines which correspond exactly to your small grid. These are the reference points which will enable you to transfer the marks from your small drawing to your final picture.

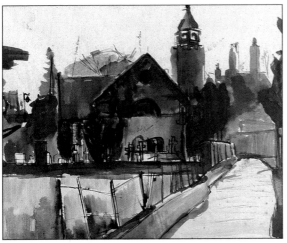

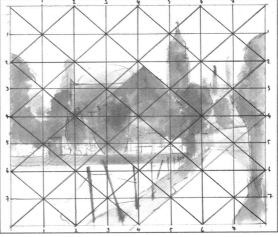

This is a pen and wash drawing made on the spot for a later painting. There are some colour notes on the actual sketch – this is often a useful addition to drawings made outside.

This small version of the original drawing has been made to improve the composition. The adjustments here are minor, mainly to give more room for the sky; this slightly increases the feeling of distance.

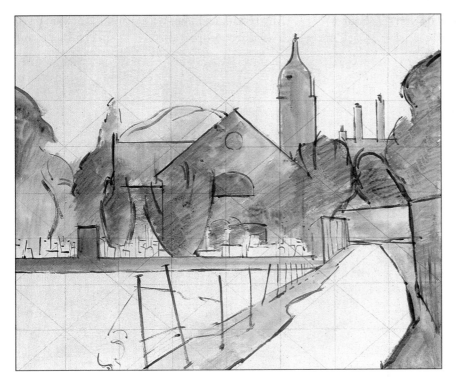

The drawing on to the support – in this case, hardboard (masonite) – has been kept very simple. Just outlining the main shapes and directions is all that is needed at this stage, the rest will come with the painting.

Composing a picture

The important thing to remember about painting is that it is not just about technical skill and knowledge. You learn and develop your skills in order to convey the excitement you feel through painting. In the first two projects I dealt with painting a picture in a fairly objective way through still life, which has involved composition, colour, and, most of all, looking. Here, I shall deal with putting together a picture from various elements to make an imaginative composition. The picture I have decided to use as an example is totally different from the previous ones in subject matter and intention. Nevertheless, the considerations which are made have a great deal in common with those involved in the first two projects.

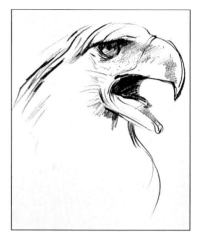

Sketchbook drawing for the eagle's head.

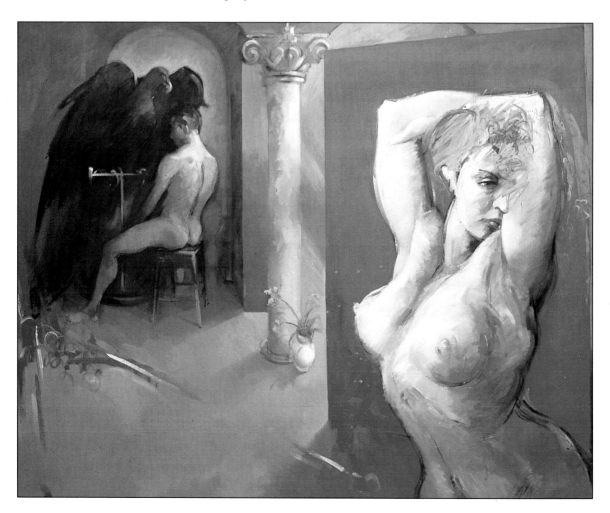

Problems of scale

The first point to note is the picture's scale and size. This picture is painted on a large format; this is an important step away from the first two pictures which were both small scale. The reason I make a point of this is that when you up the scale, there has to be much more information contained in the forms. The first two pictures were composed of small objects – fruit, and so on. Now we are dealing with large human figures – almost life size in the foreground – and a large space from front to back of the picture. The foreground figure occupies almost half of the picture space. One of the main pictorial problems was to relate the foreground figure to the background figure in a space almost devoid of objects. This has been done by the use of directional lines and points throughout the picture, and the direction of the figure's arms, which is echoed by the line of the square red shape at the top as well as the direction of the bottom line of the same red shape echoed again by the line of her breasts. These imaginary and real lines direct the eye to follow through to the seated background figure. This has to be a strong movement as each figure is contained in its own shape within the picture. This was an important aspect of the composition as the picture is about the isolation of the human figure. The curve of the bird's wing on the left of the picture is a movement to keep the eye contained in the shape. The spatial feeling is enhanced by the light tone of the foreground figure compared to the dark lost tones of the seated figure.

Choice of colour

The setting has the unreal quality of a stage set about it to give it a non-specific time and place setting. The colour is pervadingly warm, the figure in the foreground is warm in colour and tone compared to the background. To set about a picture of this nature, you need plenty of preparation. The size of the picture means that mistakes will be expensive in both time and

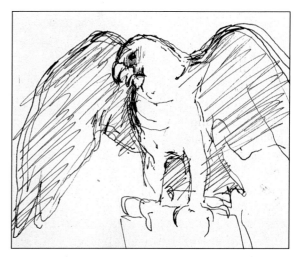

The body of the eagle.

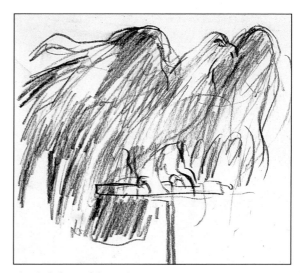

The dark form of the eagle emerging.

energy. So, a number of preparatory drawings and paintings were necessary before embarking on such a large project.

Formulating an idea

If this is an aspect of picture making that interests you there are some things which you must be sure about before you start. With still lifes, landscapes or portraits your subject is there before you and there is a direct physical link between you, but once you move away from that situation then

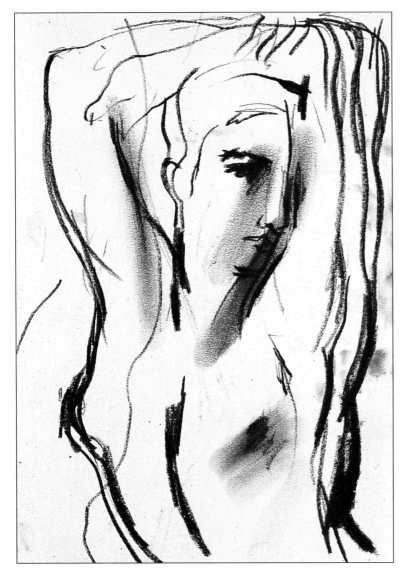

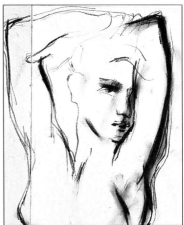

Above and left: Sketchbook drawings for the torso, defining the main directional lines.

This painting was done from life in one short sitting of about two hours. The main purpose of this study was to gather information and also to build into the painting some of the qualities that I wanted in the final picture. The approach has been kept freer than in the large picture as this is still only a study.

there are other considerations. Firstly, and most importantly, is the idea. This is the foundation of your picture. If your idea is not sufficiently strong, then no matter how well you paint it, the painting will never stand up for long, in terms of the interest and intensity the spectator requires of a painting. Having satisfied yourself that the idea merits further development then your next requirement is to gather together more than enough information about the subject or content of the picture. This could be figures, architecture,

landscape, atmosphere, or a combination of all these elements. When I say more than enough, it is necessary to be able to sieve through and discard what you don't need, rather than feel that you are scraping the barrel for information.

Painting the picture

When you have arrived at this point, then the process of painting the picture is almost the same as described for the previous projects in terms of composition, colour, shape, and line. The only

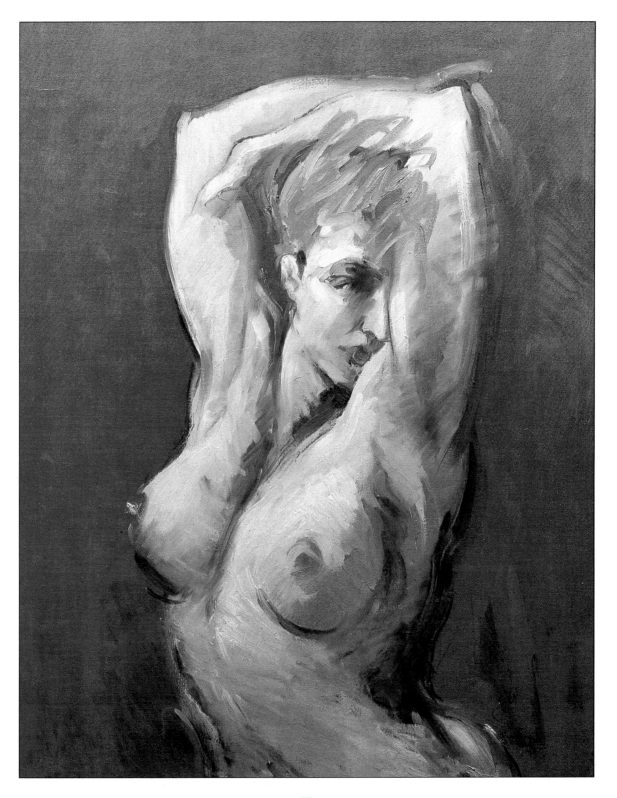

This is a sketchbook idea for parts of the larger painting, and was carried out to clarify my thoughts about the mood of the picture, rather than to make specific drawings about form and shape.

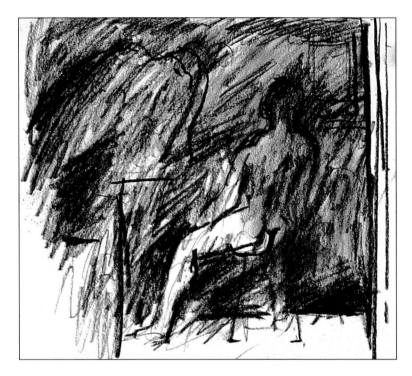

Below: This was one of many quick ideas for the painting in which colour was introduced into the sketches. These sketches are deliberately kept loose to allow for flexibility within the drawing and also to enable me to move quickly on to another sketch to develop ideas further.

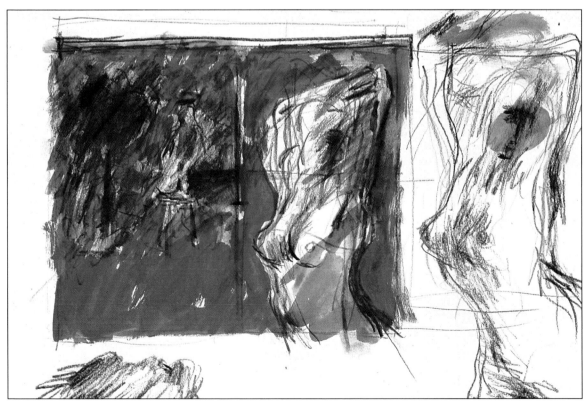

difference is that this time you can do anything with your picture – you are completely in charge. It's rather like playing with plasticine (modelling clay), you can push and pull it into any shape you like, make spaces, close them off or change scale to suit your idea. It's a wonderful feeling to have this freedom in the creative process.

There are many painters who work in this vein. Graham Sutherland, one of the great English painters of the twentieth century, merits attention. The most interesting aspect of his work for us to consider is that a great deal of his work is landscape based but composed entirely in the studio. He used landscape, and took from it various aspects, changed them and set them back down in the landscape from which they had come. There is, however, an absolute authenticity about his work, due to direct observation. He changed, composed, and re-defined shapes, but they are always believable, and the considerations of composition and colour which you have been making throughout the projects and exercises in this book relate as much to his work as they will to yours.

To learn the rules and properties of oil painting is absolutely essential to you if you are to progress and develop your talent, and at the same time, liberate your creative spirit.

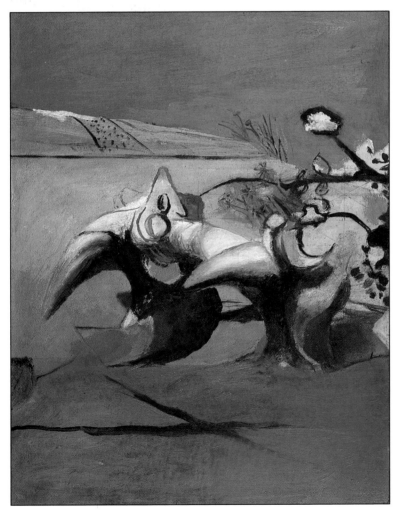

Graham Sutherland 'Horned Forms' 813 × 641mm (32 × 25¼in.). Sutherland is a painter who uses landscape rather than a painter of landscape. To use his own definition, he paraphrases landscape and forms which means that although his art is firmly based in landscape as his source of inspiration, he composes his pictures from various elements not necessarily from the same location. In this painting, one can see very definite landscape elements; the horizon line in the distance divides the sky and land mass, for example. The horned forms in the foreground have a menacing dramatic quality which, although their scale is large in the picture, probably came from quite small forms such as gorse thorns. This is essentially a picture composed of landscape and natural elements to express a particular personal feeling about an environment, and would have been arrived at through an acute personal observation using sketchbook studies and drawings.

Index

Note: Page numbers in italic refer to illustrations

acrylic primer 19, 20; *20*
'alla prima' 14, 38
Artists' colour 10; *10*

Baldwin, Martin *8*
brushes 12-13, 47; *12*
    brush care 13
    use of 24; *24*

canvas 16, 18; *17*
canvas boards 20; *16*
carrying straps 50
cartridge paper 20; *16, 20*
colour 33, 35, 38, 40, 41, 43, 44,
    45, 55; *35, 42, 43, 44*
    wheel 26; *26*
colours: mixing 27, 28; *27, 28*
composition 40-2, 46, 54-6, 59; *46*
    see also preliminary sketches
Constable, John 30, 49; *48*
cracking (crazing) 47

Daler board 20; *16*
diluents 14
dippers 15
directional lines 55; *56*
doodles 31; *31*
dragged brush techniques 30; *30*
drying times 8, 10, 11, 14, 15, 50

earth colours 10, 11
easels 15
emulsion primer 19, 20; *20*

eye levels 41-2

filberts 12; *12*

glazing 28-9, 47; *29, 47*
gloss 14
glue sizes (coatings) 18
gouache (body colour) 7
Gould, Cheryl 21
grounds 19, 38

hardboard (masonite) 19; *17, 20*
highlights 36-7, 43; *37*
Howard, Ken *38, 48*

'impasto' 7

light 34, 45, 49-50; *45*
light and dark 35, 39, 47; *34*
lighting 42
linseed oil 7, 14
Liquin 15

Master Colour 14
mediums 14
monochrome underpainting 39;
    39
muslin 20; *17, 20*

negative shapes 42

outdoor painting 49-50; *50*

paintboxes 11
painting knives 13, 30; *13, 30*
palette knives 13; *13*
palettes 14
    laying out 25; *25*
photographs, use of 51, 52; *51*

pigments 7
poppy oil 14
portraits 51
preliminary sketches 33-4; *33, 34*
preliminary studies 49, 50, 51, 55,
    56; *50, 51, 56, 57, 58*
priming a canvas 18-20

rhythm 41

scale problems 55
scumbling 31; *31*
shape 40
sketches, use of 52, 53; *53*
still life 32-7, 40-7; *32, 40*
stretching a canvas 18; *18, 19*
Students' colour 10; *10*
subject, choice of 33, 41; *40*
supports 16; *16*
Sutherland, Graham 59; *59*

texture 41, 47
    of tube paints 10
tones 35, 37, 39, 43, 44, 46; *35,
    39, 44, 46*
tube sizes 11
Turner, J.M.W. 7
turpentine 14

underpainting 38-9; *38, 39*

varnishes 47

warm and cool areas 44-5; *45*
warm and cool colours 26-7; *26*
wet into wet technique 28; *28*
Wingel 14

Acknowledgements

Swallow Publishing wish to thank the following people and organizations for their help in preparing *Starting in Oils*. We apologize to anybody we may have omitted to mention.

Unless indicated otherwise, all artwork is by the author.

Martin Baldwin, p8; Stephen Bitti p26; Cheryl Gould p21; Ken Howard pp38, 48; The Tate Gallery, London pp7, 59; Victoria and Albert Museum, London p49.

Thanks to Richmond College of Adult Education for testing the projects in this title.

The materials and equipment illustrated on pages 10-23 were kindly loaned by CJ Graphic Supplies, 35-39 Old Street, London EC1 and 2-3 Great Pulteney Street, London W1; Daler-Rowney, 12 Percy Street, London W1.